Jim & Rose,

May Parenthood be
everything you've been ho[ping]
for and more.

Love,
Jeff, Amy & Joshua

When Husband & Wife Become

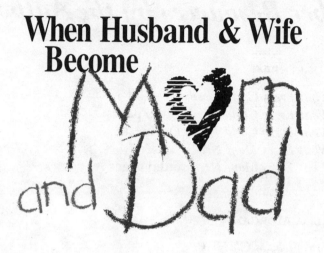

Other Resources by the Authors

TOGETHER

What Every Child Needs
What Every Child Needs audio pages
What Every Child Needs Daybreak®
What Every Mom Needs
What Every Mom Needs audio pages

ELISA MORGAN

Chronicles of Childhood
I'm Tired of Waiting!
Meditations for Mothers
Mom to Mom

CAROL KUYKENDALL

Give Them Wings
Learning to Let Go
A Mother's Footprints of Faith

What Every Marriage Needs

When Husband & Wife Become

Mom and Dad

MOTHERS OF
M♥PS
PRESCHOOLERS

Elisa Morgan & Carol Kuykendall

ZondervanPublishingHouse
Grand Rapids, Michigan

A Division of HarperCollins*Publishers*

When Husband and Wife Become Mom and Dad
Copyright © 1999 by MOPS International, Inc.

Requests for information should be addressed to:

📖 ZondervanPublishingHouse
Grand Rapids, Michigan 49530

Library of Congress Cataloging-in-Publication Data

Morgan, Elisa, 1955–.
    When husband and wife become mom and dad / Elisa Morgan and Carol
  Kuykendall
        p.   cm.
    Includes bibliographical references.
    ISBN 0-310-22698-8
    1. Parenting—Psychological aspects. 2. Man-woman relationships.
  I. Kuykendall, Carol, 1945–   .   II. Title.

HQ755.8.M64 1999
    306.872—dc21   99-39407
                                                                        CIP

This edition printed on acid-free paper.

Published in association with the literary agency of Alive Communications, Inc., 1465 Kelly Johnson Blvd. #320, Colorado Springs, CO 80920.

Interior design by Amy E. Langeler
Interior illustrations by Carolyn Fink

Printed in the United States of America

---

99 00 01 02 03 04 05 / ❖ DC/ 10 9 8 7 6 5 4 3 2 1

*To husbands and wives who
become moms and dads.*

*May your heartstrings tie
you together forever!*

Contents

Acknowledgments

This book represents the work and offering of MOPS International team members over the past decades since 1973. Our organizational purpose is to meet the unique needs of mothers of preschoolers, and one of these needs is the need for healthy marriages, so we recognized the priority of offering a resource on marriage to assist husbands and wives through their transition to mom and dad.

As in all our MOPS resources, the writing of this book has been a team effort for which many must be thanked:

—Thanks to the men and women who answered our surveys with words from their hearts. The input we received was honest, and therefore extremely helpful as we worked to accurately understand this transition.

—We are grateful to Gail Burns for her loyal efforts in typing and retyping and searching and researching our sources.

—We appreciate our readers: Karen Parks, Beth Lagerborg, and Kathleen Gregory for their input into this manuscript.

—Much gratitude to Rick Christian of Alive Communications for his advocacy of the mission of MOPS and to Sandy Vander Zicht and Rachel Boers at Zondervan Publishing House for extending this message to so many marriages.

And of course we must thank our own dear husbands, Evan Morgan and Lynn Kuykendall. After all, we first walked through this transition with them, and we've learned much of what we've written about firsthand, in partnership with these wonderful men.

Introduction

The Beginning…
When Parents Are Born

*J*ake and Abbie were about to have their first baby. They prepared the nursery, celebrated with a baby shower, read countless books, and listened to advice from everyone, including their parents, now Grandparents-in-Waiting. Still, their excitement about becoming parents jostled alongside anxiety inside their souls. Late at night they'd lie in bed together and talk about the future, their hands on Abbie's belly, marveling at every kick from their unborn baby.

They'd met just after college and quickly knew that each was the other's soul mate for life, so they got engaged and then married and dreamed about living happily ever after. Of course, they'd bumped into some problems here and there along the way, especially in the first years of their marriage as they adjusted to each other's differences and expectations, such as who does the shopping and cooking and bill paying. But now they knew each other's language of love, and they felt ready for children. Sort of. At least as ready as young couples can be when so much of parenthood looms out before you in the nebulous unknown.

Through their years of adjustment to each other, they'd fought for and found significant times of happiness. Would that happiness change? What would it be like to share their lives with a child twenty-four hours a day? What about Abbie's job? And Jake's long hours? How would they afford all the stuff a baby needs? Would they have enough love for the baby—and how much would be left over for each other? Yes, that was the most unanswered question: How would a baby change their marriage?

Weeks passed, and suddenly labor pains rushed them to the hospital with the unavoidable realization that there was no turning back. This baby was coming. *Now.*

After they checked into the hospital, Abbie and Jake struggled together for nearly twelve hours to bring a new life into the world. Finally, the doctor placed a wrinkled, wriggly, slit-eyed baby boy in Abbie's arms, and Jake leaned down to kiss his son's cheek.

This couple had become a trio. They looked into each other's tear-filled eyes, awestruck at this new life that had grown from their love. Silently they thanked God for allowing them to participate in the miracle of one of his creations. As they gazed at their baby, they had a vague awareness that they were looking into the future with a new weight of responsibility resting on their shoulders, yoking them in a partnership unlike any they had yet experienced. Jake and Abbie had created and delivered a new purpose for their marriage. The birth of their son marked the birth of a new relationship: when husband and wife become mom and dad.

WHY WE WROTE THIS BOOK

At MOPS International, an organization dedicated to helping the mothers of young children, we've been hearing a request to write something about the changes in a marriage during early parenting. Through letters, e-mail, phone calls, conversations at conventions, and in grocery stores we hear comments like these:

> What's happened to our marriage?
> My husband isn't the same person I married.
> We're more like roommates than lovers now.
> There's so little time or energy left to invest in each other.
> I have no idea how to maintain a healthy marriage since having children. I need help!

Children change a marriage—completely and permanently. They change who we are as individuals and as a couple. They both stretch and strengthen us. They throw our marriage relationship out of whack. But here's the good news: Marriage relationships can grow stronger through this wobbly period of transition as well.

Throughout this book, we'll be using the illustration of a whimsical mobile. We heard this analogy first in a classic book, *What Is a Family?* by Edith Schaeffer. She writes that a family is "meant to be a mobile, a growing, changing, beautiful art form."[1] Like most works of art, a fragile and beautiful mobile—this one in the format of a family—is constantly vulnerable to being broken.

The family mobile first comes into being at the wedding. It is made up of a husband and wife tied to each other by their heart-strings, bobbing and swaying as they adjust to each other's personalities, expectations, beliefs, and values. This wobbling is natural and eventually settles down as balance in the union is achieved. When a child is added, new strings are added, the old ones are stretched, and the family mobile once more wobbles out of whack. Again, quite normal! But this second adjustment is a bit more complicated. Now there are three lives hanging together in a pursuit of growth and balance. And then perhaps a fourth and even a fifth. Understanding these additional stresses on the original marriage unit is tricky; finding balance is a challenge.

Men and women want help understanding and coping with the transition of their marriage from husband and wife to mom and dad. This book focuses on this unique transition with clarity, help, and hope.

We wanted this book to be honest and speak to your real feelings. So we sent 1,000 questionnaires to new moms and dads around the country. We asked questions like, *What is the best—and most difficult—change you've faced in your marriage with children? Which of your wedding vows have changed in meaning since you've had children? How has the meaning of commitment changed for you? What do you need most from your spouse, now that you have children?* Openhearted answers from husbands and wives (now moms and dads just like you) are sprinkled throughout the book.

Based on the questionnaires and twenty-six years of work with moms and dads of preschoolers, we have identified six needs of marriages with young children. They are:

- Balance
- Commitment
- Interdependence
- Intimacy
- Mission
- Hope

A chapter is devoted to each of these needs, offering a definition of the need, clarification for why the need is important in the transition to marriage with children, and directions for how to meet the need in marriage. At the end of each chapter is a section called "Mobilizers." These mobilizers are included to help you and your spouse discover practical ways to meet the need discussed in that chapter and help bring stability to your marriage. The first mobilizer in each chapter is entitled "Lighten Up," since some of the imbalance in our marriages results from taking ourselves and our problems too seriously. Other mobilizers offer questions to discuss together, and still others give practical tips. All are intended to jump-start your thinking or your discussions with your spouse or in a small group.

The birth of a baby in a marriage brings about the birth of a mother and a father. Inevitably, imbalance occurs and marriages face the task of redefining who they are and how they will work now that a child is in the picture. Yes, a child changes a marriage *forever*, but married couples can choose to make the change a *good* change.

A marriage with children is a work in progress. And it is hard work. But it is a relationship with great potential to grow stronger and deeper. Understanding the transition from husband and wife to mom and dad helps establish the foundation for a fulfilling and vital marriage relationship that will endure in all the years ahead.

From our hearts to yours,

Elisa Morgan and Carol Kuykendall
for MOPS International

The Gift

We, one barren winter's morn
were blessed.
He came to us,
this confection in a blue-and-pink striped cap,
with fingers like snowflakes,
lacy and fragile,
and a bunny's nose for lips—
pink and quivering.
He came to us that day and made us parents,
joyous and afraid, elated and despairing,
and he made parents again of our parents—
and he let us see another future,
one of which we hadn't dreamed of dreaming.
And this little snowbird of ours,
this little being
who made *being* something entirely new for us,
grew in our hearts, before our eyes.
Our little snowbird,
who flies and falls and flies again,
who came to us as wisdom wrapped most carefully
in a sacred package,
who teaches himself in quiet contemplation
and loud demonstration,
our bluebird, our happiness,
our son—
how we adore this delicately balanced gift of
Heaven
and
Earth.

ANGELA S. CAIN[1]

What Marriage Needs Most

We asked husbands and wives around the country, "Now that you have children, what does your marriage need most?"

— ✻ —

Husbands said ...
Time!
Time management between us
Time away from the children
36 hours in each day and 8 days in each week
Romance
Teamwork
Spontaneity
Sleep!
Emotional closeness
Prayer
To turn off the TV
Acts of affection
Kisses, several times a day

Wives said ...
Time, time, and more time
Time alone with husband
Time alone — to myself
Bed rest
Help in sharing household tasks
To know that I'm still a desirable woman
Understanding
Affirmation
Acceptance
Sensitivity
Loving touches
Deeper spiritual commitment
Money...children are costly little people!

Best Changes
Children Bring

We asked, "What is the best change in a marriage with children?"

— ❊ —

Husbands said ...

Watching our children grow
Becoming less selfish
Being on a "mission" together
Learning not to take everything so seriously
Laughing with our children
Seeing my wife blossom as a mother
Rediscovering our own childlike joy as we watch our children make
    discoveries
Being a family

Wives said ...

Seeing my husband become a tender, loving, patient father
Experiencing the many different kinds of love
Learning to play more
Growing in our commitment from a couple to a family
Discovering another side of my husband's personality
Becoming less selfish
Learning more patience
Turning back to God

One

Balance
REGAINING BALANCE

What's happened to our marriage?

Melanie finished feeding and cuddling her five-day-old daughter and gently placed her back into the bassinet by her own bed. A glance at the clock told her it was nearly 10 A.M., so she shrugged off the urge to crawl under her comforter again. She'd better check on Kevin, who was supposed to be downstairs playing with Dad so the three-year-old wouldn't feel neglected in these first few days of adjusting to the new baby. That's one way she counted on her husband, Scott, to help out.

As she hit the first-floor landing, she heard cartoons blaring from the TV, and saw Scott sprawled out and dozing on the couch, while Kevin gawked at the screen and fingered the edge of his "blankee," a habit he'd reestablished in the last couple of days. *So much for quality time between father and son,* Melanie thought, suddenly feeling irritated.

Just then the phone rang. It was Scott's mother, who burbled on with questions about the new baby and their adjustment, and then made a statement that only fueled Melanie's growing irritation. "How wonderful to have Scott home to help you this week!" she gushed, obviously proud of her son's desire to pitch in at home.

Help? Melanie fumed silently as she looked around. Baskets of laundry were stacked in the hallway. Dishes from breakfast littered the countertops. Help? So far he'd taken in about eight hours of TV, much of that with his eyes closed. He'd told her he had to rest up to be ready to go back to work.

Mumbling something in response to her mother-in-law, Melanie hung up the phone a few minutes later. She opened the refrigerator to search for the juice Scott promised to get at the store "first thing in the morning." No juice. In fact, the grocery list was still on the counter, right where she'd left it the night before. Suddenly, something inside Melanie snapped. She put on her shoes, grabbed a jacket that nearly covered her oversized shirt and sweatpants, and picked up her purse and the list. On her way out the door, she stooped to give Kevin a hug and shook Scott to consciousness.

"I'm going to the grocery store. Alone. The baby's asleep. I'll be back in a few minutes."

As soon as she pulled her car into the street, Melanie was struck by the absurdity of the notion that going to the grocery store would calm and comfort her. What had happened to her life? For that matter, what had happened to her marriage?

At home, the hubbub of TV superheroes gradually invaded Scott's consciousness. He sat up sleepily and reached for the remote.

"Hey, Kevin, Buddy, let's get out some puzzles, okay?" Kevin dropped his blankee and scampered across the room to grab an armload of wooden cutouts. He then crawled up beside his dad on the couch.

As Scott worked the simple shapes with his son, he mused over his morning. Up at four with Jessica and then again at six with Kevin. Microwaved sausages and Cheerios for breakfast. Two calls from work. He still needed to mow the lawn and get the bills paid. Still, it didn't seem enough to please Melanie right now. Jeez, she had been a grouch a few minutes ago. But he'd come to expect these emotional roller coasters, having lived through the early weeks after Kevin's birth. He'd learned lots about parenting and marriage with children in the past couple of years. Many of his priorities had shifted because of his son, and now his daughter would surely shake them up even more.

Scott felt weary. While he loved his children, he had to admit he sometimes missed the carefree life he and Melanie used to live. Softball games with the guys, usually with Melanie attending. Going out afterward for pizza, with no worries about rushing home for babysitters. Movies not on the VCR, but in a theater. Leisurely evenings of hanging out with other couples. Freedom to make love without interruption. What had happened to his life? What had happened to his marriage?

CHILDREN CHANGE A MARRIAGE

Children. When husband and wife become mom and dad, they go through a significant transition which changes their lives and their marriage completely and permanently. For some marriages, the dramatic change begins with the first news of pregnancy. In other cases, the change is far more subtle, sneaking in slowly, hardly noticed until months after the arrival of the first or sometimes even the second child. Most transitions fall somewhere in between, but in all marriages, children change a couple and a couple's relationship in not only deeply enriching ways,

We were like newlyweds for the first nine years. Then children started arriving, three in four years. Now we struggle to maintain a relationship that is a shadow of what it once was. We are more like roommates that really like each other than like lovers. We are partners in parenting and managing our home.

— *✻* —

Suddenly our lives revolve around our child and her needs, to the exclusion of everything else.

— *✻* —

Initially, children become your marriage.

— *✻* —

Children become "Priority One."

but also in confusing, challenging ways. These changes cause a husband and wife, like Melanie and Scott, to stop and wonder,

"What has happened to our lives...what has happened to our marriage?"

Let's look at some of the ways children change a marriage.

Children Bring a Total Lifestyle Change

No doubt about it, that little bundle of joy brings a new kind of stress to the marriage relationship. Many family study experts identify the birth of the first child as a potential major crisis time in a marriage. A baby changes the roles and responsibilities of husband and wife, which means a reexamination of gender roles and a reordering of priorities, daily schedules, career goals, commitments, sleep patterns, and monthly budgets, to name just a few. Obviously, children diminish a couple's freedom and spontaneity, change a couple's sex life, social life, and friendships. Children bring a total lifestyle change.

Expect a baby to change your life forever.

— *x** —

What touches me is hearing my husband read to our preschooler ... when I know how he hates to read.

Children Bring Gifts to Marriage

Children also contribute significant gifts to a marriage. Take, for example, the entrance of a baby into the world, emerging from invisibility to suddenly snuggle into our arms as a new human being: toes and fingers, nose and eyes, hair—all uniquely blended together from the cells of our bodies. Unbelievable! Miraculous! Stunning! And it hits us that the symbol of our marital love, once a gold band of unending eternal metal, has been replaced by the creation of this new life brought forth from our union. The coming together of our life with the life of our spouse has actually brought about a new life. Adoptive parents share this same sense of wonder as they realize the noncoincidental, completely miraculous work of connecting their lives with this new baby's life forever.

Three millennia ago, the psalmist wrote that a child is a gift, and new par-

ents easily agree. As new mother Carla Barnhill observed, "God has graced Jim and me: we get to watch one of his precious children grow. We have the privilege of sharing her moments of discovery and her wonder at what she finds. She is a gift to us, one we will learn from daily. As she shows us who God made her to be, we will undoubtedly uncover more about ourselves as well."[1]

As husband and wife begin to combine their efforts in caring for their precious new child, they discover the shared experience profoundly and powerfully bonds them, as this mother's description proves:

> I remember in particular one night in my early married life when my husband and I were awakened at 1 A.M. by a very sick baby with a temperature of 104 degrees. At this point, we didn't know too much about babies, let alone sick ones, and his limp little body threw us into cooperative action. We raced to get thermometers . . . juice bottles. . . . One of us, I don't remember who, ran a tepid bath to help bring the temperature down.

> In no piece of music or brilliantly choreographed ballet have I ever witnessed such mutually accommodating counterpoint. We loved this baby. We were, for that period of time, a complete alliance whose sheer force quickly took on an identity of its own. Taking turns rocking our son, neither of us ever mentioned how tired we were; if we were, we had forgotten it. We didn't waste time negotiating ("I'll get the juice; you take the temperature."). We just pitched in together and did what had to be done for someone we both loved. . . .

> Afterwards, I remember we sat together in the kitchen and just held hands for a minute. We had been through a war. That solid, loving, victorious moment we shared as we saw our son's temperature go down and watched him go quietly to sleep was to herald thousands of moments like it that have seemed to come more quickly and closer together with each passing year.[2]

> *Children are the greatest product of our love.*

Throughout the days of marriage with children, the gifts they bring are continually discovered. A few words of caution, however. The gift of a child can't fix a broken marriage, nor does it guarantee the survival of a struggling one. Further, it doesn't "define" marriage. A marriage with children is no more a marriage than one without children. But children do bring unique gifts to a marriage that come in no other package.

Children Bring Reality to Marriage

> *Life is a blur. We take each day as it comes.*
>
> — x* —
>
> *I can't always do what I want.*
>
> — x* —
>
> *We can't do anything without first considering whether our children's needs are met.*

Children bring parents a reality check as they force us to face who we are and what we expect out of marriage and life. Fed by soap operas, movies, television sitcoms, romance novels, and even that perfect-looking couple down the street, most men and women enter marriage believing in the "happily ever after" myth that our relationship, even with children, will be filled with tender romance, fulfilling sex, quick-witted humor, and intimate understanding throughout our wedded days. Too often, love is defined by these unrealistic models.

Of course, there are wonderful discoveries of each other and shared visions for the future. But the shadowed hints of self-centeredness rarely seen in early, childless marriages can become glaring realities when children enter the scene and demand that we sacrifice so many of our own needs in order to meet theirs. Research shows that the birth of a baby brings a new closeness to couples, but it also reveals a new self-centered response to the fatigue and strain.[3]

In other words, ". . . marriages are most fragile when couples have small children, precisely the time when they need to be the most strong. A little over half of married couples report that their marital satisfaction diminished when their children arrived. Only 20 percent report that their marriage satisfaction improved after having children, while about 30 percent indicated their marriage remained the same. There are many reasons for the temporary dip in satisfaction—including conflicts over role expectations, money, work, social life—but the point is that each stage of life has different stresses and satisfactions."[4]

Witness the accusations that typically grow out of the unrealistic expectations of a couple who have become mom and dad:

- "He's simply not as helpful or attentive as I had hoped."
- "She's completely consumed by the baby and doesn't seem to recognize I'm even in the same room."
- "He hasn't had to adjust much of his life to the reality of having children, while my entire daily routine has altered."
- "She has no interest in the things we used to do together and instead wants to change or improve me."

On and on it goes. Romance? Intimacy? Fulfillment? These are the bubbles that come from soap-opera dreams, but they burst and evaporate in the real-life challenge of adjusting to the roles of mom and dad.

MARRIAGE DEVELOPMENT 101: CHANGE IS NORMAL!

The fact is, just as marriages naturally grow and change as we go through transitions in life, so does the way we experience and express our love for each other. The romantic passion of new love eventually grows into the stage of comfortable love, which grows into the stage of deeply committed love. And in between are inevitable times of numb love or dull love or quiet

> *Life changed, and nothing has been the same since. With growing children, we're constantly in transition.*
>
> — 🌸 —
>
> *I am sick to death of marriage self-help books that say "you can rekindle the romance" in your marriage by dating or some other quick, little solution. We are different people from when we first met and were engaged. So the nature of our love has changed.*

love. Years ago, *The Saturday Evening Post* ran an article on "The Seven Ages of the Married Cold," which humorously traces the seasons of marriage through the reaction of a husband to his wife's colds during the first seven years of marriage.

Year One: "Sugar Dumpling, I'm worried about my baby girl. You've got a bad sniffle and there's no telling about these things with strep throat around. I'm putting you in the hospital this afternoon for a checkup and a rest. I know the food's lousy, but I'll bring your meals in from Rossini's."

Year Two: "Darling, I don't like the sound of that cough; I've called Doc Miller to rush over. Go to bed like a good girl, please, just for Papa."

Year Three: "Maybe you'd better lie down, honey. I'll bring you something to eat. Have we got any soup?"

Year Four: "Look dear, be sensible. After you feed the kids and get the dishes washed, you better hit the sack."

Year Five: "Why don't you get yourself a couple of aspirin?"

Year Six: "Why don't you gargle with something instead of sitting around barking like a seal?"

Year Seven: "For Pete's sake, stop sneezing! Whatcha trying to do, give me pneumonia?"[5]

As newlyweds, most of us fervently pledge that "we will be different!" We will stay in the "Year One" category. And yet, years later as we care for a colicky infant or incessantly demanding toddler, we suddenly discover that we, too, have less patience for the needs of our spouse and that our marriage has begun to match the descriptions of "older" marriages.

In the book *Passages of Marriage*, the maturity of a marriage is discussed. "The developmental stages through which a child passes from birth into adulthood are well known. Similarly, a marriage matures from developmental stage to developmental stage—from passage to passage—according to the number of years it has existed."[6] Five such passages are identified:

> **Young Love:** first two years, overcoming the idealistic notions of marriage and molding two individuals into one unit, a family.
>
> **Realistic Love:** 3rd through 10th year, recognizing the subconscious reasons you married your spouse, the hidden agendas and secret contracts.
>
> **Comfortable Love:** 11th through 20th years, establishing and maintaining an individual identity along with your marriage identity.
>
> **Renewing Love:** 21st through 30th years, grieving and accepting the inevitable losses of your marriage.
>
> **Transcendent Love:** 31 years and thereafter, unveiling new reasons for existing after the major life tasks of achieving financial security and nurturing the next generation have been completed.[7]

As a marriage moves from passage to passage, it will encounter crisis and conflict, deepening and growing as it endures.

HANG IN THERE

Hope comes in realizing that the chaos you're experiencing in your marriage is perfectly normal. The birth of a child does bring an imbalance to your relationship, but here is the important message: You can regain your sense of balance in your marriage by recognizing this as a normal transitional change and learning how to love your way through this transition. In fact, the way you and your spouse regain your balance as you face this challenge will establish the pattern you will use to face other developmental changes in your marriage in the future. Learning to love your way through these normal periods of imbalance will deepen and enrich your marriage relationship.

We went from being very close to being too tired to talk.

Mobilize Your Marriage

Remember the description of the mobile in the introduction? As we said, marriage is like one of those whimsical mobiles, often hanging above a child's bassinet. Picture the following marriage mobile. On one side is the husband and on the other is the wife. They are joined together in a permanent bond by a string of wedding vows that attach each to the other—heartstrings, if you will. In the beginning, when it is just the two of them, this bond is strengthened as they learn to live attached rather than unattached, and work at fulfilling the common purpose of marriage: union.

As time goes by and they grow to understand each other better and become more familiar with the experience of attachment, husband and wife establish a balance in their mobile marriage relationship.

But when a change occurs with one person in the mobile, it affects the other. Imbalance results, and the couple wobbles around until a sense of balance can be regained. A job change for one partner swings and dips the other as well. An illness for one bounces the other around. A difficult relationship in the extended family blows at the marriage mobile and causes chaos. But while these circumstances affect the marriage mobile, the adjustment is temporary because the circumstance causing the imbalance is temporary.

When a child is attached to the marriage mobile, however, it causes an imbalance that requires a more permanent adjustment. Both husband and wife actually experience a major role change as their very identities are altered and they become mom and dad. No longer is life about "you and me," since baby makes three. And the baby is often the most powerful and highest priority. Someone said it well with this quote, "A perfect example of minority rule is a baby in the house."

Regain Balance

Regaining balance comes as we begin to understand some basic principles regarding marriage.

First, marriage is alive. Marriage is like a living organism. It is not stagnant; rather, it grows and changes and adapts as it goes through the seasons of life and as the individuals grow and change. The health of the relationship, in fact, depends on this ability to adjust and grow as we stretch beyond ourselves to embrace the new part of both of us and our relationship. We need to adjust our attitudes and see change as good.

Instead of seeing marriage as a soap-opera romance, stuck forever in the first season of young love, we need to understand that our relationships will evolve through time, and look forward to this necessary growth. Writing on "The Discipline of Love," Anna B. Mow says "the fiction writer's mistake [is] in thinking that a couple could ride along on the love that they started out with, instead of having to grow in love."[8]

Marriage also endures inevitable periods of boredom. Elizabeth Cody Newenhuyse, in an article entitled "Are We Still in Love?" writes:

> Sooner or later, married partners need to come to grips with the reality that there are worse things than being bored. Our culture has seduced us with the lie that life should be continuously exciting, varied, stimulating. . . . Yet periods of dullness are inevitable in a marriage of any duration. Dry periods will be followed by renewal. Sometimes, though, it takes awhile. But it *will* change.[9]

Second, marriage can hurt. Contrary to so many of our expectations, the most loving relationships can also be the most painful. So often a couple is surprised to discover pain in a marriage relationship, fearing that pain means something is wrong.

The truth is, loving another deeply always comes with a cost, and that cost often involves pain. In the closing scene of the movie *Shadowlands*, C. S. Lewis muses that pain is part of the joy of loving. In other words, the people we love the most and those who love us the most can cause us the greatest pain.

According to Roberta Temes, a psychotherapist and assistant professor of psychiatry at Downstate Medical School in New York City who regularly consults with couples seeking divorce counseling, "...there is pain in being single, in being married, and in being alive. Marriage does, however, provide a person to blame for pain."[10]

The initial imbalance brought by the arrival of a child into a marriage relationship can bring about anxiety, uncertainty, fear, frustration, anger, insecurity, and a myriad of other emotional realities that can all be lumped under the category of "pain." No, things aren't the way they used to be; they are different. And different is not comfortable for most of us. Different means getting up when we used to be able to sleep comfortably through the night. Different means coming home on time because someone needs us, when we'd rather linger away from responsibilities. Different means swinging out of balance in our marriage mobile and yearning deeply for the restoration of balance.

> *Marriage with children is so much harder than I thought it would be. It is wonderful, too, and we love our children dearly, but we live in a constant state of physical exhaustion, financial strain, and emotional stress. There is little of us left to invest in our marriage.*
>
> — *x* —
>
> *The pressures, stresses, fatigue, and busyness of life increase with children. It takes more effort to maintain a marriage relationship.*

Third, marriage is work. Balance can't be restored by going back to the way things used to be. Balance only comes by gaining understanding and acceptance in the present with how things are now. Psychologist and family therapist H. Norman Wright suggests that five issues are important in the early season of marriage in which husband and wife are becoming mom and dad:

- Defining the roles of husband and wife.
- Creating a new relationship with parents.
- Transforming romantic love into a love based on steady commitment.
- Beginning a family and establishing roles as parents.
- Settling into an established personal identity and pouring energy into what has been identified as important: career, family, friendships, or priorities.[11]

We waited so long for our firstborn that we put our total focus on him. It's taken us a while to see ourselves as a couple again.

Marriage is hard work because you are constantly learning new things about yourself and your spouse. You are constantly trying to adapt by seeking self-improvement ... or falling short and feeling guilty! As authors William and Nancie Carmichael observe, "Married love is hard work because it requires us to constantly think of our spouse instead of ourself, and our natural bent is to think of ourself first."[12]

THE GREATEST GIFTS YOU CAN GIVE YOUR MARRIAGE AND YOUR CHILDREN

Is seeking balance worth it? Of course. Successfully negotiating the transition from husband and wife to mom and dad is the greatest gift a couple can give to each other in marriage. When you learn to "hang in there" with each other, and to understand each other's moods and responses to the transition of children, you are establishing a stronger bond and deeper relationship. Each adjustment acts as an investment in each other and in your marriage that will bring dividends of deeper satisfaction in the years ahead.

As Dale Evans Rogers wrote: "When two caring people who are committed to each other wrestle with the inevitable hard times that confront every married couple, in a spirit of kindness and tenderness and forgiveness, miracles do happen."[13]

When you learn to "hang in there" with each other, you are also giving a priceless gift of loving security to your children. A familiar bit of advice on parenting is directed to both mom and dad: "The best thing you can do for your children is to love each other." Children are watching us all the time, and when we model a relationship that hangs in there through life's normal conflicts and challenges, we are demonstrating to them that they, too, will have a place to hang securely in life, despite everyday difficulties. Marriage teaches us how to love, and children learn that lesson from watching.

CONCLUSION

According to most parents, life with children is richer but harder. But the attitude with which we approach this transition has lots to do with the way we regain our balance. Greg was completing his degree in clinical psychology and Erin was a labor and delivery nurse when they reflected on their new roles as parents.

> When we had our daughter, our lives did change, but it wasn't the negative type of change others were talking about. People had us so worried that life as we knew it was over. We clearly remember driving home from the hospital thinking, "Yesterday was our last day of freedom!" Had we maintained that belief, then that day would have been our last day of freedom. Since the birth of our daughter, our lives have changed for the better because we learned how to balance being a parent and a spouse.[14]

While all couples seek balance in marriage, we will, inevitably, face periods of imbalance. The key is to recognize that imbalance in marriage is normal—and then begin the process of loving our way back to balance again.

MOBILIZER #1: LIGHTEN UP

Children Change Us!

Once babies discover their feet, they love to grab their toes. Removing a sock becomes a game. Keara played with her socks and I read. After a few minutes, she started gurgling and laughing. I looked up at her and saw that she held her little yellow sock in her hand. It was her first catch. A proud moment. She tilted her head a bit, looked straight at me with a "watch this" kind of expression, and placed the sock on her head. She sat there staring at me with the sock on her head and the goofiest expression on her face, waiting for me to respond. I laughed with more spontaneity and joy than I'd felt in months. She took the sock off her head. Then she gave me the look again and put it back on. I laughed so hard my ribs hurt. Tears cascaded down my face. Again and again, she took the sock off and then put it back on her little bald head. And *every* time, I laughed more than the time before. . . .

When my husband called that afternoon, I immediately burst out laughing. Keara was sitting in the infant seat beside me. Given my track record over the previous months, Brian thought I was sobbing.

"What's wrong?" he asked with alarm.

"Brian," I gulped, "Keara . . . *put a sock on her head!*"

"And? . . ." Brian asked while I laughed hysterically.

"Oh . . . that's it. . . . It's just that she put this yellow sock on her head and it was . . . so unbelievable funny."

As if she knew what was happening, Keara put the sock on her head again.

"Oh . . . she's doing it again!" I cried. I couldn't contain myself.

"Well, that's good . . . I guess," said Brian tentatively. "Why don't we talk about it when I get home?" He was probably mentally calculating whether we could afford for me to see a therapist.

I was laughing so hard I couldn't say good-bye. I became Keara's mother that day. And she became my child.[15]

MOBILIZER #2: MAKE YOUR OWN MOBILE

Why not make your own mobile to serve as a whimsical "visual aid" or reminder to hang in there together when your marriage gets wobbly and out of balance?

Here's a simple set of instructions with materials you may have around the house. Picture the kind of colorful, swinging mobiles you sometimes see in a baby's nursery and improvise to create a similar one. You'll need:

- Something to represent the number of people in your house. Cookie cutters, children's toys, or even cutout cardboard figures will work. Aluminum gingerbread cookie cutters are perfect because you'll find them in different sizes and they are easy to string together.
- Ring: A main attachment piece from which to hang the mobile. You could use a strong metal or plastic ring, an old bracelet, a shower curtain ring, a loose-leaf binder ring, or a metal coat hanger, twisted to the desired configuration.
- A couple of wooden dowels or something from which to hook or tie the mom, dad, and children together.
- Ribbon, string, or yarn to tie the mom, dad, and children together.

Directions: Tie them all together, as in this drawing.

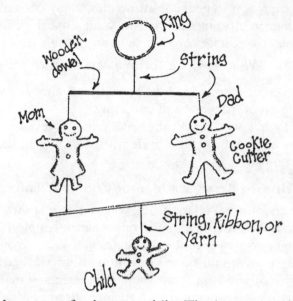

P.S. If you're not crafty, buy a mobile. The important thing is to hang the mobile where you and your spouse will both see it, a reminder to both of you of the way a married couple wobbles around, sometimes out of balance, but always hanging together.

MOBILIZER #3: FIND A MENTOR COUPLE

Whimsical mobiles are not the only visual aids helpful to a marriage with children. So are the examples of other couples who are farther down the road of marriage than you are. Why not find at least one couple you both admire and make them your "mentor couple"? The arrangement can be as informal or formal as you like, but the idea of mentoring is one of the oldest and most effective ways of passing knowledge and skills down from generation to generation. Besides, many of us didn't grow up with great examples of what we want a marriage to look like, and a mentor couple could serve as an encouraging model.

What to Look for in a Mentor Couple

- People who are at least several years ahead of you on the path of marriage and parenting.
- People who reflect the same values you do.
- People who have a style of warmth, genuineness, and empathy.

How to Arrange a Mentor Couple Relationship

In an informal relationship, you and your spouse can benefit from merely identifying potential mentor couples. This might include your own parents or couples you knew growing up. If they are people you both know now, observe them and then discuss what you appreciate about their style and manner, especially with each other and with their children.

In a more formal relationship, you could ask one of these identified couples if they would meet with you, maybe once a month for an hour, over coffee or dessert, to share insights and perspectives. If they agree, come to those meetings with specific questions or concerns you've had. Assure your mentors that you don't expect them to have all the answers or be perfect, but that you appreciate their stories of their own experiences. By merely having survived the imbalances of marriage in the early parenting years, they are examples of success to you. Their descriptions of working through difficult times will give you hope.

MOBILIZER #4: TEN KEYS TO KEEP YOUR NEW BABY FROM DRIVING YOU APART

1. "The greatest thing parents can do for their children is to love each other," advises Dr. Benjamin Salk, family psychologist.
2. Be careful about protecting your own privacy, while still giving your baby as much love as you can. Keep a balance between commitment to each other and to your children.
3. Have conversations with your spouse that are not dominated by the latest in baby food and teething rings.
4. Realize how easy it is for the father to feel both unneeded and excluded.
5. Share as many tasks as possible, even if this means they are not done to perfection. The baby will survive with a crooked diaper.
6. Recognize how physically shattered many women become with the sheer effort of looking after a small baby.
7. Try to show intimacy in other ways if sex is not at the top of the agenda for a while. Make sure this is not confused with rejection.
8. Don't lose touch with your friends.
9. Let trusted friends look after your child for a few hours so you can go out as a couple.
10. Keep a sense of moderation in terms of your child's involvement in extra activities. As he or she grows, you can exhaust yourselves and your child quite easily. Ask yourself how important it is that a six-year-old take ballet lessons, play soccer, and practice three musical instruments.

In summary, from the day they are born, get ready for the day when they will leave. It happens so fast it'll take your breath away. If you don't prepare for that day, in eighteen years you will come home some evening, sit down to eat, look across at your spouse and say, "Who are you?"[16]

MOBILIZER #5: LOVE BUSTERS—RECOGNIZE AND ELIMINATE THEM!

Here are five descriptions of things couples do, often unwittingly, which make each other unhappy. These "love busters" exist in most marriages, and—even though we do them at our partner's expense—they somehow bring us a subtle sense of comfort. For a healthy marriage, we should seek to recognize these behaviors and commit to overcome them. They are:

1. **Angry Outbursts.** Anger usually occurs when someone is making you unhappy and what they're doing just isn't fair. Anger offers a simple solution to a problem—destroy the troublemaker. If your partner turns out to be the troublemaker, your anger will urge you to hurt the one you've promised to cherish and protect. But when anger wins, love loses.

2. **Disrespectful Judgments.** Have you ever tried to "straighten out" someone? We usually think we're doing that person a big favor, lifting him or her from the darkness of confusion into the light of our "superior perspective." But if you try to straighten out your spouse, to keep him or her from making mistakes, you are making a much bigger mistake. It is a disrespectful judgment.

3. **Annoying Behavior.** One of the most annoying things about annoying behavior is that it doesn't seem all that important—but it still drives you bananas! You should be able to shrug it off, but you can't. Try to divide annoying behavior into two categories: If behavior is repeated without much thought, it is an *annoying habit*, such as the way a person eats or talks or leaves the cupboard doors open. If it is usually scheduled and requires thought to complete, it is an *annoying activity*, such as sporting events or a personal exercise program. If you want compatibility in your marriage, get rid of that annoying behavior now.

4. **Selfish Demands.** Demands depend on power and carry a threat of punishment. Ideally in a marriage, there is shared power—the husband and wife working together to accomplish mutual objectives with mutual agreement. But when one spouse starts making demands, along with threats that are at least implied, then power is no longer shared. As a result, the threatened spouse often strikes back. Suddenly the marriage is a tug of war, a test of strength. Who has enough power to win? When one spouse wins and the other loses, the marriage loses.

5. **Dishonesty.** No one likes dishonesty, but sometimes honesty seems more damaging. What if the truth is more painful than a lie? Lies clearly hurt a relationship over the long term, but truth can also hurt, especially in the short term. Many couples continue in dishonesty because they feel they can't take the shock of facing the truth, at least right now. As a result, the marriage dies a slow death. Honesty is like a flu shot. It may give you a short, sharp pain, but it keeps you healthier over the following months.[17]

MOBILIZER #6: THE MARRIAGE KILLERS

- **Overcommitment and physical exhaustion.** Beware of this danger. It is especially insidious for young couples who are trying to get started in a profession or in school. Do *not* try to go to college, work full-time, have a baby, manage a toddler, fix up a house, and start a business at the same time. You *must* reserve time for one another if you want to keep your love alive.

- **Excessive credit and conflict over how money will be spent.** Pay cash for consumable items or don't buy. Don't spend more for a house or car than you can afford, leaving too few resources for dating, short trips, babysitters, and so on.

- **Interference from in-laws.** If either the husband or wife have not been fully emancipated from their parents, it is best not to live near them. Autonomy is difficult for some mothers (and fathers) to grant, and close proximity can mean trouble.

- **Space invaders.** Aliens from Mars are of no concern; rather, the concern is toward those who violate the breathing room needed by their partners, quickly suffocating them and destroying the attraction between them. Jealousy is one way this phenomenon manifests itself. Another is low self-esteem, which leads an insecure spouse to trample the territory of the other. Love *must* be free, and it must be confident.

- **Pornography, gambling, and other addictions.** It should be obvious to everyone that the human personality is flawed. It has a tendency to get hooked on destructive behaviors, especially early in life. For some there is a weakness and a vulnerability that is unknown until they become addicted to something that tears at the fabric of the family. Their problems often begin in experimentation with a known evil and ultimately end in death . . . or the death of a marriage.

- **Business failure.** It does bad things to men, especially. Their agitation over financial reverses sometimes sublimates to anger within the family.
- **Business success.** It is almost as risky to succeed wildly as it is to fail miserably in business. The writer of Proverbs said, "Give me neither poverty nor riches, but give me only my daily bread" (30:8).[18]

MOBILIZER #7: THOUGHTS ABOUT MARRIAGE, CHILDREN, AND CHANGE

Marriage—as its veterans know well—is the continuous process of getting used to things you hadn't expected.

TOM MULLEN[19]

Most of us become parents long before we have stopped being children.

MIGNON MCLAUGHLIN[20]

People change and forget to tell each other.

LILLIAN HELLMAN[21]

The best marriages, like the best lives, were both happy and unhappy. There was even a kind of necessary tension, a certain tautness between the partners that gave the marriage strength, like the tautness of a full sail.

ANNE MORROW LINDBERGH[22]

Questions to Ask Each Other

- How is our marriage different now that we have children?
- What is the most difficult change we've discovered in our marriage since having a child?
- What is the best change we've found?
- What gifts does our child bring to our marriage? How does a child deepen our love for each other?
- What couple do we know who is a good role model for our marriage with children? Why?
- What is "married love" and how is it different from other kinds of love?
- What can we do to regain balance in our marriage relationship?

Recommended Reading

Forever My Love, Neil Clark Warren
Happily Ever After . . . and 21 Other Myths About Family Life, Karen Linamen
Love For All Seasons, John Trent
Marriage 911, Becky Freeman
Marriage Moments, David and Claudia Arp
Seasons of a Marriage, H. Norman Wright
The Strong Family, Charles Swindoll

Two

Commitment

RECOMMITTING YOUR LIFE

Will you love me even when it's hard?

Rhonda rolled over in her bed and groaned ... a barely audible, involuntary groan that awakened her from a restless sleep. Her stomach churned, her face felt flushed, and her body ached. For a moment she lay still, trying to assess her condition without waking her husband. Then suddenly she bolted from the bed to the bathroom in the darkness. A wave of nausea shook her body, and it responded, violently.

She pulled the door to the bathroom behind her, embarrassed by the sounds of her illness, but soon she heard a soft knock, and the door opened slightly. "Honey, are you okay?" her husband, Jim, asked through the crack.

"I'm sick," she moaned, as she lay in a heap on the floor of the bathroom. She felt dizzy, and the room swirled around her.

All at once she felt strong hands lift her and help her back to bed. A wet washcloth was placed on her forehead and a tissue dabbed at her mouth. From somewhere down the hall, she heard their two-year-old daughter, Melissa, whimpering, "Mommy ... Mommy." She wanted to respond, but she couldn't make her body move. A few minutes later, she heard the bedroom door softly close, and she realized that Jim had gone to their daughter.

Several days later, when Rhonda felt better, she began more fully to comprehend and appreciate the significance of her husband's actions that night. He had *seen* her throwing up! Ugh!

Not only that, he had gone, in her place, to comfort their daughter and had discovered her in a puddle of her own illness.

For the first time in their married life, both she and the baby were sick at the same time, and Jim had taken care of both of them. He mopped up the messes, changed Melissa's sheets and pajamas, cleaned her up with tissues and a washcloth, and then created a cot for himself on the carpeted hallway between his "girls'" bedrooms. As it turned out, he didn't get much sleep, as he spent most of the night moving between one room and the other with towels and buckets and thermometers.

Rhonda wrapped the memory of Jim's tender and loving actions around her like a huge blanket and nestled into its comfort. Since the birth of Melissa, their marriage had been tested in many ways, and she'd often wondered if Jim would love her and be there for her, no matter what. Even when she felt impatient and grouchy at the end of a long day with Melissa. Even if she never lost those fifteen post-pregnancy pounds. Even when she climbed into bed at night and wanted to sleep more than she wanted to make love. The memory of Jim's selfless actions on the night of the "family flu fiasco" gave her an answer she would cherish always.

PROMISES, PROMISES

You learn what "for worse" means when you've both had a long day and the kids are screaming.

*— ɔ** —*

Commitment is lived out in caring for a newborn around the clock, no calling in sick, no substitutes, no sleeping on the job. A great lesson in commitment.

*— ɔ** —*

Commitment is what I need when I don't feel like being committed.

"For richer or for poorer." "In sickness and in health." "Till death us do part." We stand at the altar and offer our promises in our vows to one another, having hardly a clue about the depth or meaning of those words, or the gutsy kind of action required to keep them.

Minister Joy Jordan-Lake describes marriage vows as "outrageous words." She describes the journey of bride and groom toward the altar saying, "They have lived, these two, not even a third of their lives, maybe not a quarter, yet they parade past long pews of soundlessly cheering crowds towards promises they have understood only well enough to say yes to—but not well enough to understand what living that yes means. . . ."[1]

Living out the "I do's" of our wedding vows "until death do us part" is what commitment is all about. It means being there for that other person, not only through the starry-eyed days of new love, or the storybook setting of a wedding, or the romantic honeymoon, when loving is easy and feels good. It means living out those vows when the bills come in, when PMS strikes again, when a job change means moving to an unfamiliar city far away, when loving *doesn't* feel good. Commitment is not based on feelings; it is based on the determination to survive together—no matter what. This concept is described in *A Mother's Footprints of Faith:* "Love starts with romantic feelings but marriages are built upon a choice of commitment as two people learn to live out their wedding vows and the description of love found in 1 Corinthians 13, which might have been read at their wedding."[2]

Commitment is about keeping your promises to each other. It is the foundation of a strong marriage, and it grows and changes through the years and seasons of life.

HOW DO CHILDREN CHANGE COMMITMENT?

Let's go back to the analogy of the marriage mobile. In the beginning, the bond of commitment links only husband and wife. However, when a child is added to the mobile, the bonds of commitment are stretched to include a third person. Consider, for instance, the story about Jim and Rhonda and the "family flu fiasco." When Rhonda got sick before they had a child, Jim could take care of her without sacrificing much of his time or sleep. His commitment stretched to meet the needs of only one other adult. But when a child entered this picture, and

I didn't understand total commitment until we had kids. I was totally committed to our marriage for life. But that was easy compared to being a wife and mom. I want to be great at both, but only have so much to give. Most days I feel overcommitted!

— *x** —

Commitment to my wife now involves commitment to kids.

both Rhonda and the baby were sick at the same time, Jim's commitment to love his wife "in sickness and in health" changed considerably. The act of living out this commitment required a greater personal sacrifice of time and sleep. The fact is, children change a marriage, and change the way we live out the commitment of our wedding vows.

Children Complicate Commitment

Commitment to a spouse means working things out with another, mostly independent, reasoning adult. It means giving time to one person. It means combining incomes and compromising needs and wants on everything from how to spend a Saturday afternoon to menu choices for dinner. Still, it's not so hard to take turns when one wants grilled chicken and another prefers pasta.

As the story of Jim and Rhonda illustrates, children complicate all those choices and require greater compromises. The addition of a child involves the readjustment of schedules, an inevitable delay of date nights, and settling for fast-food carryout meals several weekends in a row. We might start out the beginning of the day with our spouse in mind, but somewhere between breakfast and Barney, we forget the other while focusing on our toddler. Commitment is far more complicated in a marriage with children. In facing and making choices and sacrifices, we realize we can neither *have* it all or *give* it all.

Children Deepen Commitment

In a very positive way, children mature and enrich the meaning of commitment. Life isn't just about "us" as a couple anymore; it's about "us" as a family. Together, a couple is committed to the new goal of raising a child, and must help each other in that common goal.

> *Every time we say no to an outside commitment, we say yes to each other.*

Husband and wife must fight against the temptation to meet his or her own self-centered needs—for sleep or time alone or new possessions—to instead consider carefully what is best for the baby, both now and in the future. A husband gives up an afternoon of football because his wife needs a break. He knows it will help her be a better mom, which in turn helps the child. A wife quits talking to her husband about her desire for a new sofa because she knows the money needs to go toward a new stroller and car seat. The couple's commitment matures and deepens as both discover they are able to give far more than they ever dreamed possible.

Children Test Commitment

By the same token, children also test commitment as husband and wife face the daily challenges of living out the vows made at the altar. "In sickness and in health" includes a child when a husband or wife has to cancel a meeting to make an unscheduled trip to the doctor. The test of commitment may transfer to the other spouse when he or she has to cancel plans in order to stay home with a flu-ridden family.

> *I thought our lives would go along like a fairy tale, "happily ever after." But after sickness, job loss, and many other bumps in the road, I realize that enduring is what marriage is all about.*
>
> — ✻ —
>
> *The phrase "love and cherish" has changed its meaning for me. I used to cherish my wife solely out of love. Now I cherish her not only because of love but because of her needs as a mother.*

Parenting together also reveals differences in dealing with conflict or discipline issues that sometimes threaten commitment to unity in marriage. When we have children, we are tested about what really matters, about how determined we are in our commitment to each other.

Yes, children complicate, deepen, and test the commitment of marriage as they stretch it beyond the boundaries of husband and wife to include the whole family. This stretching causes an adjustment, and though we don't always respond as lovingly or patiently as we'd like in this adjustment, our sense of commitment to each other and to our marriage is strengthened in the stretching.

WHAT *IS* COMMITMENT IN MARRIAGE, ANYWAY?

I did not think about our wedding vows prior to having children. With the new stresses in our relationship, I understand why they were included in the ceremony.

To understand the life-altering, lifelong nature of this stretching in a marriage with children, let's look more carefully at the meaning of the marriage commitment, and how it grows and changes. A marriage commitment is threefold.

First, Commitment Is a Promise

From the time we are little, we learn that a promise means "keeping our word." The dictionary defines a promise as a "declaration assuring that one will or will not do something." In a marriage ceremony, we commit ourselves to the promise that we will live out our wedding vows. Most commonly, this promise is made in a church before a minister, which signifies that the promise is made before God. It is also made, most commonly, in the presence of family and close friends. In many wedding ceremonies, the minister will ask the bride and groom to turn around and face the people attending. "Take a good look at these people," the minister says solemnly, "for they are the ones who will remind you of the promises you are making here today."

In marriage, a couple commits to a promise to hang together for a lifetime. Always. Through all seasons and changes. At twenty-four, such a promise means one thing. At thirty-five, it's another. And at fifty-two, it's grown to yet another thing. But in every season, commitment is a promise to grow and accept and work at being there for each other. It is a promise to *not* throw in the towel. It is a promise to not divorce.

> *We went into marriage totally committed, knowing that the word divorce would not be spoken, much less an option. However, our children call on us to prove that over and over.*

Elizabeth Sherrill writes about the power of the marriage promise as she reflects back on her fifty-year-old vows to her husband, John. "Promises are scary things," she says. "To keep them means relinquishing some of our freedom; to break them means losing some of our integrity. Though we have to make them *today*, promises are all about *tomorrow*...."[3]

The promise of commitment a couple makes at their wedding in the *todays* before children is played out as quite another promise in the *tomorrows* of being parents. Anna B. Mow stretches us to think of living out our commitment to each other moment by moment, just as we live out our commitment to God: "Our life of commitment to God is made up of minutes, just as our commitment to one another in marriage is made of minutes, stretching into a lifetime. Each moment is an important part of the whole."[4]

Second, Commitment Is a Promise to a Person

A promise made in marriage is a commitment to a specific person, a promise about the priority of that person in your life and the role you will play in that person's life. It is a promise to "bond" together, which is identified as a vital ingredient of long-term marriages in the classic book, *Love for a Lifetime*, by Dr. James Dobson. As Dobson reminds us, "Bonding refers to the emotional covenant that links a man and a woman together for life and makes them intensely valuable to one another. It is the specialness that sets those two lovers apart from every other couple on the face of the earth."[5]

Author Tim Kimmel characterizes married love as a commitment to a person in this way: "Love is the commitment of my will to your needs and best interests, regardless of the cost."[6] In short, it's pledging to your spouse, "You come first for me, and I'm committed to living out that priority today. I also know that investment will make a difference for good or for ill tomorrow."

For many in marriage, such a resolve grows slowly and not without major effort. A person's resolve also experiences a natural ebb and flow in the seasons of a marriage. Philip Yancey writes,

> Before marriage, each by instinct strives to be what the other wants. The young woman desires to look sexy and takes up interest in sports. The young man notices plants and flowers and works at asking questions instead of just answering monosyllabically. After marriage, the process slows and somewhat reverses. Each insists on his or her rights. Each resists bending to the other's will.
>
> After years, though, the process may subtly begin to reverse again. I sense a new willingness to bend back toward what the other wants—maturely this time, not out of a desire to catch a mate but out of a desire to please a mate.... I grieve for those couples who give up before reaching this stage.[7]

How vital is this aspect of commitment! To *say* we are committed to our spouse is one thing; to *act out* that commitment is another thing entirely. As psychologist John T. Gossett puts it, "Commitment is not just something people say. It's how they act. Is this person the most important part of your life or not? If so, then lots of other good things follow. If not, then lots of good things cannot take place."[8]

Commitment to a person is not based on feelings, but on an intentional act of the will. Author C. S. Lewis points us on the right track when he writes,

Every inch, nook, and cranny of my life is now filled with demands. My job, my time, my sleep, my energy, my finances. Commitment is important.

Love . . . as distinct from "being in love" is not merely a feeling. It is a deep unity, maintained by the will and deliberately strengthened by habit; . . . (a couple) can have this love for each other even at those moments when they do not like each other. They can retain this love even when each would easily, if they allowed themselves, be "in love" with someone else. "Being in love" first moved them to promise fidelity; this quieter love enables them to keep the promise. It is on this love that the engine of marriage is run; being in love was the explosion that started it.[9]

Third, Commitment Is a Promise to a Person Who Is Your Partner

This third element of commitment in marriage is uniquely applicable to those who have children. In the truest sense, all marriages are partnerships. When two become one, they unite body, soul, and spirit to-

Raising children can cause differences of opinions, but we are committed to staying together.

ward the common goal of living and loving together for a lifetime. They partner, for instance, to make a home together, including shared decisions about furnishings, decorations, and what goes where. They often share the responsibilities of hospitality in their home, as well as decisions about finances and budgeting. They may even share a business. They might join in extended family caretaking. A couple *partners* in many ventures from the common ground of their marriage.

The God-given task of parenting has deepened the "I do's."

Marriages that partner in the process of raising children experience one of the strongest forms of partnership. Husband and wife experience a heightened awareness of mutuality as they become parents and begin to partner in the shared goals of raising children, the responsibilities of caring for children who are dependent and needy. They join together in the task of providing a legacy and future for their offspring, which they hope will outlast their presence on earth.

THE REWARDS OF COMMITMENT

In our world today, we all hunger for the assurance and security that we are loved and accepted. Mother Teresa sums up this universal longing when she says, "The biggest disease today is not leprosy or tuberculosis, but rather a feeling of being unwanted, uncared for and deserted by everybody. The greatest evil is the lack of love."[10]

Henri Nouwen, priest and author of books on the contemplative life, seconds that opinion with the observation that "much of our pain comes from our experience of not having been loved well."[11] In our heart, we yearn for the security that comes from being loved well. We want to be utterly convinced that we are loved unconditionally, no matter what, by at least one other person. And that's probably the greatest reward for sharing commitment in a marriage.

According to the Bible, both marriage and families were created by God as a primary place for relationships to grow and thrive. In our society, marriage and the family are intended as safe and secure havens for growth and nurturing. Therefore, a marriage with commitment offers a relationship with great potential.

Commitment Provides Security for Spouses

As Gary Smalley puts it, "A plant must have sunlight if it is to flourish and be healthy. In marriage, providing a deep sense of security for your spouse is like bathing her or him in warm sunlight. Every enduring marriage involves an unconditional commitment to an imperfect person. That commitment involves convincing your spouse in a variety of ways that, no matter what, you will always be available for her or for him."[12]

> *I need the security of knowing my husband loves me and that my needs are important.*
>
> — *x* —
>
> *Commitment means knowing my husband loves me even though my body's not what it used to be—I don't have to feel ashamed.*
>
> — *x* —
>
> *I like being known so thoroughly and still accepted so deeply.*

This is not a take-each-other-for-granted kind of security, but the kind that surrounds the spouse with a knowledge that "I am loved for who I am," because that's what you've promised to do. It's the kind of security that means "I don't have to prove myself to you," a security built on trust and respect.

Writer Nicole Wise cites benefits of commitment in marriage in providing emotional security for the spouse, saying, "It gives you both a place in your life that's uniquely yours, apart from the demands of work and children. And because making your marriage number one has to be a joint project—it's not something one partner can achieve through reading an article or book—it's a way for you and your husband to become more intimate."[13] Commitment in marriage also brings security against divorce and the power of the threat that word carries.

Philip Yancey confesses, "Our second year together, when the word *divorce* slipped into arguments as the ultimate trump card, we agreed to disarm that power. We promised never to wield the word as a threat or a weapon. I am glad."[14]

Commitment Provides Security for Children

As we've stated, the best thing we can do for our children is to love our spouse. Children gain a deep sense of security from knowing their parents love each other and will hang in there together, no matter what. The model of commitment children see in their parents' relationship serves as a rich source of confidence and assurance. Children even thrive on seeing their parents appropriately put their marriage above the children. Psychologist John Rosemond argues against attending to a child at the sacrifice of the marriage, which he claims ". . . turns families upside down, inside out, and backward."[15] Commitment also safeguards children from the fear or pain of divorce. As Gary Kinnaman writes in his book *Learning to Love the One You Marry,* "If you ever come to the place where you think you're trapped in a miserable marriage, you've only seen the beginning of sorrows. Just get a divorce, and you will compound the suffering, for you and for everyone else in your family."[16] Conflict is real and unavoidable in marriage. But children gain the greatest degree of security when their parents commit to stay and work through the conflict.

No matter how many times we tell our children we love them, it won't mean much if they don't see us loving each other as an example.

— ✻ —

I'm ready to leave, but I won't because of the children.

WHAT IF COMMITMENT IS ONE-SIDED?

What if you have read this chapter and the words don't seem to apply to your marriage because you are committed but you fear that your spouse is not? What if you seem to care more about the future of your relationship than your spouse does? Or maybe you have grown and changed since your child was born, but your spouse has not. Or your spouse has changed in a way that concerns or even frightens you. What if you are beginning to wonder if you married the wrong person? Where do you turn and what do you do in the midst of these painful questions?

Do Not Lose Hope

Don't give up. As we've said before, all marriages go through transitions, and both husband and wife may not adapt to the changes at the same time or on the same level. It takes work and patience and prayer to regain a sense of balance in your relationship.

In his best-selling book *Getting the Love You Want*, Harville Hendrix describes how many modern marriages function as a box. You choose a mate, climb into your box together, settle in, and then take your first close look at your boxmate. If you like what you see, you stay in the box; if you don't, you climb out of the box and look around for another mate. Or you stay in the box together, tighten the lid, and put up with an unfulfilling, disappointing relationship for the rest of your lives.

Hendrix offers another solution:

> I propose a more hopeful and, I believe, more accurate view of love relationships. Marriage is not a static state between two unchanging people. Marriage is a psychological and spiritual journey that begins in the ecstasy of attraction, meanders through a rocky stretch of self discovery, and culminates in the creation of an intimate, joyful, lifelong union. Whether or not you realize the full potential of this vision depends not on your ability to attract the perfect mate, but on your willingness to acquire knowledge about hidden parts of yourself.[17]

Obviously, the word *willingness* is the key here, because you or your mate may not be *willing*. But many couples who have faced and survived crises in their marriages will tell you that change came not from changing their mates, but from changing themselves. So there is hope in learning more about the "hidden parts of yourself," especially as you seek resources to help you. There is also hope for you in the other chapters of this book, as you learn about interdependence, intimacy, mission, and hope.

Talk to Your Mate

This is so obvious, you're probably responding with "Duh. Of course." Yet many married people deny or suppress their concerns about commitment rather than face their mate with them. Common guidelines for effective communication apply here. First, find a good time and safe place to talk. This means away from the distractions of children and phones and televisions. If at all possible, plan the date ahead of time. Maybe a Saturday morning breakfast at a coffee shop; maybe an overnight, if you can work out the details. Second, communicate your concerns honestly and clearly. (Maybe your "talk" has to be on paper in a letter because you express yourself best in written form.) And third, be willing to listen just as openly to your mate's response.

Be Strong

In his book *Love Must Be Tough*, James Dobson addresses the problem of disrespect in marriages that are drifting toward divorce. He offers practical advice to the partner who desperately wants to hold the marriage together and advocates a loving toughness rather than a pathetic pleading sort of response. He claims that begging or anger or guilt only lead to the other spouse's increased feelings of being trapped. When love becomes an obligation rather than a privilege, the less committed spouse experiences an even greater desire to escape. Instead of trapping the partner, Dobson suggests using a stronger, more confident approach of "opening the cage door," or pulling back and offering the partner some space. Often, the emotionally distant partner then moves closer to his or her spouse rather than farther away.[18]

Find Help

In a crisis with a one-sided commitment, the committed spouse is not able to handle the challenge without outside help. If you are in a one-sided marriage, resist the urge to downgrade your spouse or get involved with spouse-bashing to a friend. Instead, channel concerns in a direction where real help is available. Help can be found in books and resources, but also through people in your community—a pastor, an older couple or person who will mentor you, or a counselor who comes with a good recommendation.

RECOMMITTING YOUR LOVE

The word *commit* is a verb. It's something we *do* over and over again. When a baby is added to the marriage mobile and everyone feels stretched and out of balance, a couple has to redefine their sense of commitment to strengthen their stretched bonds. This requires individual determination on the part of both husband and wife.

Neil Clark Warren underlines the value of this individual determination in his book, *Forever My Love*. He stresses:

> Commitment is more than "sticking it out." It requires a far more active approach in marriage—and certainly during a time of marital challenge. It's active rather than passive. . . . There are . . . huge promises that you make to your spouse— all of which are highly active, all of which involve only *your* action, all of which make you unilaterally and unequivocally committed for as long as you live—no matter what![19]

The over and over again need for commitment is really a *recommitment*, which restores balance to the marriage mobile.

> *I can't solve my wife's problems. But I can listen sympathetically.*
>
> — x* —
>
> *"For better or worse" seems more real to me now. Kids add to the "for better," but they also have made the "for worse" times harder.*

The decision to keep recommitting is not based on feelings but on a couple's determination to keep the promise of their marriage vows to each other. Janis Abrahms Spring, author of *After the Affair*, writes, "Most people wait for love to return before they'll recommit to their marriage. I say just the opposite—the couple has to recommit to the marriage *before* love will return."[20]

Recommitment in marriage comes through intentional efforts in four areas.

Sacrifice

In the 1800s, Ralph Waldo Emerson remarked that "the greatest gift is a portion of thyself." His comment is as true today as it was more than a hundred years ago. Sacrifice means choosing to put the needs of your spouse first above your own. As Gary D. Chapman puts it, "The element that lifts marriage to its highest potential is the attitude and the practice of service."[21]

Sacrifice is wrestling your body from sleep to care for a crying baby so that your spouse can rest. It's giving up your moment of free time to wash dishes or clothes or cars or babies without being asked. It's offering the last bite of pie to your husband or choosing the less comfortable chair so that he can stretch out and have the couch all to himself. It's giving your wife the car with the best snow tires and heater. Sacrifice means giving up a bit of your comfort to bring comfort to your spouse.

Kindness

Les and Leslie Parrott, marriage counselors and new parents themselves, write, "Kindness is an integral part of love because it stems from an uncalculating attitude that desires neither monetary payment nor human applause. . . . Kindness is love's readiness to enhance the life of another person."[22]

Sounds similar to sacrifice, huh? Well it is, *kind of.* Sacrifice sets aside our need for the need of our spouse. Kindness doesn't necessarily require a sacrifice; it is simply a small behavior that enhances the life of the one we love.

Kindness brings a cup of coffee to the bedside of your spouse. It calls up a babysitter and whisks a wife away for an unexpected dinner out. It takes a phone message for a husband when he's napping on Sunday afternoon. It notices the way you look and offers a compliment. It says "please" and "thank you" and "I love you."

Forgiveness

He barbecued all the hamburgers to well done—again—even though you like medium rare. She railed on you for not spending more time with the kids. He couch-potatoed the afternoon away, not even noticing that you were cleaning the entire house and keeping the kids quiet. She spent more money at the mall when she promised she wouldn't. He didn't even get you a card for your anniversary. She seemed tired and disinterested in your advances. In the irritations of the everyday moments, marriages are maintained only with liberal doses of forgiveness, which restores balance as no other action can.

Forgiveness doesn't hold grudges. It aims to move beyond the disagreements. It doesn't major on the minors. It doesn't get stuck in trivial mistakes. As Vicki Huffman suggests, "Forever-love . . . accepts the reality of the past but lives beyond the blame game."[23]

Discipline

Love is perfected only through the discipline of practicing the habits that will make your marriage work. Like any other skills, these habits improve with practice. Richard Foster defines discipline as "the ability to do what needs to be done when it needs to be done." In making the recommitment of marriage work through the changes of having children, a husband and wife need to practice the daily disciplines of sacrifice and kindness and forgiveness. By making these disciplines work in small ways, they are able to use them when they are needed in larger ways as well.

As a couple, you might want to identify other disciplines you know you must practice in your continual recommitment to each other and to your marriage. For instance, you might agree to not criticize each other's family members or use "hot-button" comments like, "You are just like your mother (or father)." You may agree not to retreat into silence during a conflict. You may agree to phone each other when one of you will be more than half an hour late. And once you have committed to these agreements, discipline yourselves to stick to them.

CONCLUSION

Strong, enduring marriages are built on strong commitments to hang in there and love each other through all the changing circumstances of life; to grow and change together, as husband and wife *and* as mom and dad. It is a commitment to learn to love the way God calls us to love.

Many couples use 1 Corinthians 13:4–8 in their wedding ceremony because it is a passage that gives us God's definition of love. The words become the plumb line of perfect love, against which we measure our relationship. In attempting to live out this definition of perfect love with all our human imperfections, we obviously fall short. Still, we can see these words as something to aim toward with commitment to grow and change and learn to love better:

> Love is patient, love is kind. It does not envy, it does not boast, it is not proud. It is not rude, it is not self-seeking, it is not easily angered, it keeps no record of wrongs. Love

does not delight in evil but rejoices with the truth. It always protects, always trusts, always hopes, always perseveres. Love never fails.

1 Corinthians 13:4–8

As we commit ourselves to love in this way, we should not make choices based on what *feels* good, but based on our determination to live out that commitment.

As James Dobson says, "It is not enough to make a great start toward long-term marriage. You will need the determination to keep plugging, even when every fiber in your body longs for (something else). Only then will you make it to the end. But hang in there . . ."[24]

MOBILIZER #1: LIGHTEN UP

A Lighter Look At How Commitment Cools

Here's a piece often copied in local newspapers over the years:

> A woman accompanied her husband to the doctor's office. After his checkup, the doctor called the wife into his office alone.
>
> He said, "Your husband is suffering from a very severe disease, combined with horrible stress. If you don't do the following, your husband will surely die."
>
> "Each morning, fix him a healthy breakfast. Be pleasant, and make sure he is in a good mood. For lunch make him a nutritious meal. For dinner prepare an especially nice meal for him. Don't burden him with chores, as he probably had a hard day. Don't discuss your problems with him, it will only make his stress worse. And most importantly, make love with your husband several times a week and satisfy his every whim. If you can do this for the next 10 months to a year, I think your husband will regain his health completely."
>
> On the way home, the husband asked his wife what the doctor had to say about his condition.
>
> "He said you're going to die," she replied.

MOBILIZER #2: RECOMMIT YOURSELVES TO EACH OTHER—OVER AND OVER AGAIN

Review Your Vows

On your wedding day, you repeated some important vows to each other. Can you find those vows? If not, write them out so you can review them year after year.* Consider how your commitment to each other has grown and changed, and how you have come to understand those commitments at deeper levels. Keep recommitting yourselves to each other, especially as you grow and change. Or, as Anne Ortlund says, "Get married over and over—but always to the same person."[25]

*If you can't find your own vows, here is a sample of some vows from a traditional ceremony, with wording to help you recommit your vows to each other:

> Minister: "Friends, we are gathered together in the sight of God (and in the presence of this congregation) to join (again) in holy matrimony, which is instituted by God. Let us therefore remember that God has established and sanctified marriage and declared that a man shall leave his father and mother and cleave unto his wife. By His apostles, He has instructed those who enter into this relation to cherish a mutual esteem and love; to bear with each other's infirmities and weaknesses; to comfort each other in sickness, trouble, and sorrow; to provide for each other, and for their household; to pray for and encourage each other; and to live together as the heirs of the grace of life. It is therefore not to be entered into lightly and unadvisedly, but thoughtfully and reverently. (*Here may be a prayer.*)
>
> "Will you continue to have ___ to be your wife, to live with her in marriage? Will you love her, honor and keep her, in

sickness and in health, and faithfully keep yourself to her alone, as long as you both shall live?"

Husband: "I will."

Minister: "And, ___ , will you continue to have ___ to be your husband, to live with him after God's ordinance in the holy estate of marriage? Will you love him, comfort him, honor and keep him in sickness and in health, and faithfully keep yourself to him alone, as long as you both shall live?"

Wife: "I will."

Husband's vow: "I, ___ , will continue to keep you, ___ , as my wife; to have and to hold from this day forward, for better, for worse, for richer, for poorer, in sickness and in health, to love and to cherish, as long as we both shall live."

Wife's vow: "I, ___ , will continue to keep you, ___ , as my husband; to have and to hold from this day forward, for better, for worse, for richer, for poorer, in sickness and in health, to love and to cherish, as long as we both shall live."

(If the husband is putting the ring on her finger.)

Husband: "This ring I give you again in token and pledge of our constant faith and abiding love."

(If the wife is putting the ring on his finger.)

Wife: "With this ring I wed you again in the name of the Father and the Son and the Holy Spirit."

Minister: "Wither you go, I will go; where you lodge, I will lodge; your people shall be my people, and your God, my God."

(Here there may be another prayer, followed by a kiss and some sort of celebration.)[26]

Analyze Your Vows

If you analyze the traditional marriage vows, you will discover six separate parts:

1. I will love you as long as we both live.
2. I will cherish you as long as we both live.
3. I will honor you as long as we both live.
4. I will be for you everything that a husband or wife owes to their spouse.
5. I will never give my love to, or get romantically involved with, another person.
6. I will do all five of these things under every kind of condition for as long as we live.[27]

Rewrite Your Vows in Your Own Words

Here's a "for instance":

*   I will be with you, no matter what happens to either of us, as long as we both shall live.
*   If you lose your job, I'll be there.
*   If you become disabled in any way, I'll be at your side.
*   When we're angry at each other, I promise to believe it will work out, and stand with you anyway.
*   When we get bored with each other, I will commit myself to keep working at making it better.
*   When things are great I'll be there, too, so that all our successes may be shared successes.[28]

Remind Yourselves of Your Wedding Day

Don't keep your wedding pictures tucked away in an album. Sprinkle a few framed wedding pictures around your house or establish a grouping of them in your living room or bedroom, places where you will see them often and remember your wedding day and the vows you promised each other.

At every wedding you attend together, hold hands, listen to the vows, and get remarried again.

MOBILIZER #3: RECOMMIT YOURSELVES TO KINDNESS

When you first met, remember how you loved to give each other daily doses of kindness, little gestures that said "I love you"? Rekindle that habit. Here are some ideas to get you thinking:

"Golden Rule" It

The purpose of marriage is mutual ministry, not manipulation. God brings two people together so that he will be glorified through their demonstration of love for each other and others.

One way we can begin to exhibit the kind of love that speaks highly of God is through "golden-ruling" your spouse. In what is probably the most-quoted verse in the Bible, Jesus says, "Love your neighbor as yourself." Applying this commandment to marriage, we might say, "Do for your spouse what you'd like done for yourself."

What does that mean? Well, figure out what you'd like your spouse to do for you and then do it for him or her. A survey of marriage partners revealed these suggestions:

- Praise me when you like what I did.
- Bring me a cup of hot chocolate on a lazy Saturday.
- Take the kids to the park so I can have some time alone.

Other Acts of Kindness

Here are some other acts of kindness that may require sacrifice and service to each other, but that are evidence of the commitment that lifts your marriage to a higher level.

- Measure out the coffee the night before and set out two coffee cups.

- Establish your own sign language that says "I love you." Use it often.
- Say, "Go back to sleep, honey. I'll get the baby."
- Be the first to change the stinky diaper.
- After the kids are in bed, clean the kitchen together.
- Go along on an errand, just for the ride.
- Go to the grocery store together; split the list and race to see who finishes first.
- Say "I'm sorry" quickly, whenever necessary.
- Notice each other . . . a new haircut, a cut on a finger, new shoes.
- Be polite to each other, in front of your children and others.
- Stand up for each other.
- Listen, really listen, with your eyes and face and brain and ears.
- Fill the car with gas when you know your spouse will be the next to drive it.
- Acknowledge the kind gestures you receive. Say "thank you."
- Be kind to his or her parent when they telephone.
- Make sure you each have "lunch money" after a trip to the ATM.
- Bring in fresh towels while your spouse is showering.
- Remember special projects your spouse is working on and ask how they are going. Take a real interest in what your spouse is accomplishing or struggling with.

MOBILIZER #4: LOVE IS . . .

Taking off from the verses in 1 Corinthians 13, here are some new "Love is . . ." definitions. Compare each to the original found in the conclusion of this chapter. What do you think of each definition?

Love is. . .
> slow to suspect (quick to trust)
> slow to condemn (quick to justify)
> slow to reprimand (quick to forbear)
> slow to belittle (quick to appreciate)
> slow to demand (quick to give)
> slow to provoke (quick to conciliate)
> slow to hinder (quick to help)
> slow to resent (quick to forgive).[29]

MOBILIZER #5: REMEMBER YOUR LOVE STORY—AND RETELL IT OFTEN

How did you and your spouse meet? What were those first few days or months like? Get out your wedding pictures on every anniversary and talk about your wedding. You'll be asked to repeat the story of your romance many times in your life, especially to your children, so think about the details. Write it down so it will outlive you. Here are some questions to get you started:

- When did you first see your spouse?
- What made you look a second time?
- What attracted you to each other in the beginning?
- Where did you go on your first date?
- What was your favorite song together?
- What was your favorite date?
- How did your families and friends respond to your "new love"?

- What were some "acts of kindness" you shared during your dating days? Chocolate chip cookies, notes on windshields, a knitted sweater?
- What pet names did you call each other?
- When and how did you get engaged?
- What was unusual about your wedding?
- Where did you go on your honeymoon, and why did you choose that place?
- What do you love more about your spouse today than when you got married?

MOBILIZER #6: COMMITMENT BRINGS SECURITY

Your commitment to each other brings a sense of security to your relationship. Here are some ways to increase security in your relationship:

- Say "I love you" regularly.
- Drop the word *divorce* from your vocabulary.
- Make long-range plans together.
- Cultivate a pattern of truthfulness.
- Value each other's thoughts and feelings.
- Demonstrate a strong commitment to Christ and to the spiritual health of your family.

MOBILIZER #7: STRATEGIES FOR SAFEGUARDING YOUR MARRIAGE COMMITMENT

Here is a summary of one couple's commonsense, pro-marriage choices:

- **Work at keeping your marriage fun and fulfilling.** A marriage characterized by growing intimacy and trust, coupled with the playfulness of a good sex life, is a combination anyone would be foolish to jeopardize. Work at developing mutual interests. "Creeping separateness" (the tendency to be so engrossed in our own activities and interests that we have less in common with our spouse) can be a marriage killer.
- **Commit to mental fidelity.** Most of us, at some time or other, will be attracted to someone other than our spouse. This in itself isn't sinful; we're sexual, emotional beings who have the ability to form attachments to others, especially with those whom we work closely or see frequently. The key is how to respond: Think about, fantasize about, and involve yourself with that other person, or redirect that sexual energy toward your spouse and marriage.
- **Refuse to take unnecessary risks.** Reduce the odds of temptation by evaluating each business, ministry, and social opportunity to make sure it supports your marriage. That sometimes means bowing out of after-hours business functions where spouses aren't included, or suggesting alternatives more beneficial to our marriage.
- **Stay alert to subtle dangers.** Stay informed of societal trends which help you understand the dangers. For instance, researcher George Barna in his book *The Frog in*

the Kettle, takes this trend a step further. He predicts that by the year 2000, "Americans will really believe that a life spent with the same partner is both unusual and unnecessary." You simply cannot afford to go along passively with these societal trends that threaten your marriage. Work at shoring up your defenses on the home front, keeping yourselves mentally faithful, refusing to take unnecessary risks, and boldly uphold a different standard.[30]

MOBILIZER #8: LEARN TO LOVE

Train Our Love

Train our love
that it may grow
slowly . . . deeply . . . steadily;
till our hearts will overflow
unrestrained and readily.
Discipline it too,
dear God;
strength of steel
throughout the whole.
Teach us patience,
thoughtfulness,
tenderness and
self-control.
Deepen it
throughout the years,
age and mellow it
until,
time that finds us
old without,
within,
will find us
lovers still.

RUTH BELL GRAHAM[31]

Questions to Ask Each Other

- What does commitment mean to us?
- How has having children changed our sense of commitment?
- What has been the easiest wedding vow to live out?
- What has been the most challenging wedding vow to live out?
- How have we experienced the rewards of commitment?
- What are some "acts of kindness" I could do for you?
- How can we act out a recommitment of our love today? On our next wedding anniversary?

Recommended Reading

Boundaries in Marriage, Henry Cloud and John Townsend

The Five Love Languages: How to Express Heartfelt Commitment to Your Mate, Gary Chapman

Gifts You Give One Another, Willard Harley Jr.

The Heart of Commitment, Scott Stanley

Hedges: Loving Your Marriage Enough to Protect It, Jerry Jenkins

How To Bring Out the Best in Your Spouse, H. Norman Wright and Gary Oliver

Love for a Lifetime, Dr. James A. Dobson

Love Is . . ., Les and Leslie Parrott

Making Love Last Forever, Gary Smalley

What If I Married the Wrong Person? Dr. Richard Matteson with Janis Long

Three

Interdependence
REDISCOVERING YOUR RELATIONSHIP

Who are you and me now that we are three?

Ben hung up the phone with a sigh, cleared off his desk, and gave a word to his assistant as he left the office. On the drive home, he wondered why the phone call had bothered him as much as it did.

His wife had called, pinched for time. Their almost three-year-old was in that in-between stage where he needed a nap but didn't want one. Andrea had a big meeting tonight—she was on a gallery's board of directors— and hadn't found any time to prepare. So she called Ben.

It wasn't that Andrea had interrupted him in the middle of a project, because his current project wasn't due for a few weeks. He wondered if it was because she had asked him to come home early to help.

As he pulled into the driveway, Ben was still mulling over the matter. One step into the house and Andrew assaulted him. "Daddy's home!" he shrieked as he hurled himself toward his father, tackling him about the knees with a leg hug. "How's my man?" Ben asked, scooping up his son and airplaning him through the family room to the kitchen where Andrea cradled the phone on her shoulder while stirring a pot on the stove. Half-made somethings were spread across the counters, along with splotches of flour and sugar. Papers and files and letters were scattered across the kitchen table. *Geez, what a mess,* Ben thought.

Andrea kept talking into the phone, but rolled her eyes at Ben, as she pointed at her watch with a panicked look. Ben kissed her forehead and sat down at the table, with Andrew giggling and squirming to get out of his father's arms. In the confusion, the piles of paper on the table went flying in every direction.

"Ben!" Andrea hissed at her husband as she placed her hand over the receiver. "I thought you came home to help! I had those all in order!"

"Didn't look like much of an order to me!" Ben responded defensively.

Andrea scowled and then spun around to continue her phone conversation. Ben ordered Andrew to calm down and began gathering up the papers on the floor.

Funny, he thought, *Andrea didn't used to be so disorganized.* He remembered back to their early days of marriage when she held down a career and seemed to enjoy managing the groceries and cooking and homemaking. He'd always respected her ability to handle so many things at once. Actually, he still respected her—immeasurably—but things had changed. A child had changed them. Andrea was a great mom . . . but things seemed out of control sometimes.

And why did he have to come home to help? His mom would never have asked his dad to leave the office early to help her out. But then, his mom didn't serve on boards and consult with businesses on time management. What would his dad say if he knew Ben was home playing with his toddler at 3:20 on a Wednesday afternoon while his *wife* worked? Ben wondered who he was becoming.

Andrea finally hung up the phone and rushed over to the table where Andrew was about to attack the papers again. "Ben, please! Go play with him so I can get something done!"

"What's for dinner?" Ben asked as Andrew left the room to fetch some toys from the family room.

"I don't know," she said, removing a pan of muffins from the oven. "You'll have to figure it out. But don't touch these. They're for my meeting," she said.

"You know, you could have started all this earlier and then you wouldn't be in such a mess right now," Ben offered.

"Ben, I appreciate you coming home, but I don't appreciate your lecture on managing my time. All of my time is spent managing Andrew! You forget, *I* don't have an assistant anymore, like you do. I used to be in control of when and how I did everything. Now I don't have any time to *finish* anything. And I have to *ask* you for help. Your life hasn't changed much in the last three years, but mine has changed completely." Tears filled her eyes and she wiped them away. "Sometimes I wonder who I'm becoming."

PARENTING CHANGES WHO WE ARE

When a child is born, a mother and a father are born as well. This new title totally changes who a husband and wife are, individually and as a couple. In many ways, the change is wonderful as husband and wife are enlarged and enriched by their new identity as parents. In other ways, they are challenged to understand the confusing changes in themselves and their partners. In fact, one of the ongoing challenges of

> *I felt like my husband's life didn't change much and neither did his needs. My life changed completely ... my schedule, my friends, my priorities. It was frustrating to figure it all out and try to explain it to him in a good, not angry, way.*
>
> — x* —
>
> *Having children brought us closer as a "team." Our personalities balance one another's.*
>
> — x* —
>
> *The best change in becoming parents is watching my wife change into a mother, and me change into a father, and watching our love for each other deepen.*

marriage is to constantly know and accept and keep up with the growth and changes. Let's look at some of the ways a child changes a husband and wife.

We Change as Individuals

Becoming a mom or dad changes who we are as individuals. Think back to the concept of the couple in the marriage mobile, connected to each other and hanging together in a balanced configuration. When a child is added to this mobile, husband and wife now are tied to this child as well, which creates a new configuration. The original balance of the two-way union is thrown off.

For the wife, the change is both physical and emotional; these two people are inexplicably woven together. Her body is no longer her own, but actually becomes womb, nest, and food dispenser for a child. Her involuntary physical response to her child shocks her in its intensity. Her milk flows at the sound of her child's cry, even in the middle of the shopping mall. At night, she bolts from deep sleep to complete consciousness at the sound of her baby's soft whimpering. Instinctively, she reads the meaning of that cry, and adjusts her reaction accordingly. Her heart experiences an invasion of a new kind of consuming, protective love. As Katherine Hadley puts it, "The decision to have a child is to accept that your heart will forever walk about outside of your body."[1]

Not all of these changes are welcome, nor do they confine themselves to the neat little boxes of our lives where they first appear. Slowly the changes spill over into all areas. For example, the physical changes often affect a woman's self-esteem. One mom describes how her body changed from thin to overweight, resulting in an issue of identity:

> Pregnancy and breast-feeding became "license" for me to eat. It was wonderful! They afforded me an excuse to eat whatever I wanted and the clothing to hide the fat in! . . . I lost hope of ever being slender again. I stopped caring about

my self and devoted myself completely to the children. They were a source of pride and joy to me—feelings I no longer had about myself.[2]

I love seeing my wife's joy in being a mother.

For the man, the change of identity is more gradual and often more external. On finding his wife pregnant, he alternately stoops under the heavy financial role being a parent will require, and then struts with pride at his reproductive prowess. He will have a family! After witnessing the miraculous birth of his baby, he marvels at his response to both wife and child. The child promises him a future he'd never much considered. And his wife—wow! How incredible that she can do this "birth" thing! The instinctive hunter-gatherer part of him rises up to protect and provide for his new family.

Then he is struck with the reality of what he doesn't know and can't do. He wonders, "How does she *know* what cry means 'I'm wet' or 'I'm hungry'?" He concludes that his wife has some mysterious gifting for parenthood that he lacks. On the one hand, he hates leaving for work in the morning; he might miss something extraordinary in the development of his child. Yet on the other hand, he is thrilled to be set free from this confusing world of newborns. As the years pass, he continues to explore his role as father, taking cues from his memories of his own father and other males around him, and then testing out his assumptions on his own turf. Some attempts succeed; others are met with resistance from his wife. Sometimes a trickle of doubt runs through his mind as he wonders who he is becoming, and whether he has the stuff it takes to be both husband and father.

We Change as a Couple

As alarming as the individual identity changes can be, the changes to the husband and wife as a couple can be even more

> *My husband doesn't know how to help me. When I express a problem, he wants to instruct me on how to solve it. I don't want him to solve it; I want him to listen.*
>
> — *x** —
>
> *We get too independent when we spend too much time apart.*

startling. Psychologist H. Norman Wright observes, "The birth of a child tests the identities of both parents. Husbands and wives by this time have found ways to build their identities through success in certain performance-oriented tasks, jobs, or skills. When the child arrives, the qualities they feel they possess are soon tested."[3]

The roles and identities we created in our marriage are bumped and sway wildly through these transitional days.

Ah, yes, the wife is "taken over" with her love for her child. Yes, she feels alone, terrified and overwhelmed by the unendingness of the task before her, and she struggles to know how to ask her husband for help. This is a new request, one that often creates a new, uncomfortable kind of dependence and tension. And as much as she needs her husband, she doesn't want to be touched; she's constantly touched by her baby and needs some physical space and freedom. She doesn't always understand herself as her hormones yo-yo. When she tries to express her needs, they come out in a confused tangle.

As the months and years go by, she adjusts to the responsibility of a baby, but she finds that most of her time is taken over by the child, and then by subsequent children, if she and her husband have more. Where she used to be in control of her schedule, now her children are in charge. Perhaps she used to work full-time in a challenging career and now she has left it to be a home-based mom. She struggles with isolation and the sometimes unchallenging tasks of potty training and the same-old daily tasks. Or she might still be active in an occupation—whether as a volunteer or for pay—and she wrestles with stretching her energy and time to cover the bases. She occasionally views her husband with resentment for his freedom to come and go as he pleases.

I'm 99 percent mom and 1 percent me.

In her article in *Ladies' Home Journal* entitled, "Why'd I Marry Him, Anyway?" Melinda Marshall expresses such typical mom-emotions.

> I'll have been called home from work by the school nurse to take Kathryn, who's just spewed all over the cafeteria, to the pediatrician's along with her two brothers, for whom I have no alternative care. We'll be sitting there in the waiting room, the children clawing each other's eyes out, me plotting how to conjure dinner from a fridge full of condiments, when suddenly I wonder, "What good are husbands, anyway?"[4]

For the husband, marriage after children is different as well. After a child arrives, the woman he loves is attached to another human being so intimately and intricately that the man sometimes feels—almost irrationally—left out. He watches his wife consumed by feeding and nurturing another person with the devotion she once offered to him alone. Why does he feel jealous?

And then he's baffled by her emotions. When she expresses her needs, he wants to quickly get to the bottom line and fix the problem, so he offers advice and then discovers that she doesn't want a solution; she wants sympathy. He tries to remember how his father handled his mother in such moments, but when he applies similar tactics, they usually backfire. He misses the intimacy of his wife's

My husband knows me well, but I don't think he understands me.

— ✳ —

My wife provides the compassionate side of our partnership.

companionship and the spontaneity of making love whenever and wherever they desired.

Then both husband and wife are growing and changing in other more subtle ways with the new responsibility of parenting. One is thinking totally differently about priorities; one is feeling a renewed need to go to church. One is changing a viewpoint about politics and public schools and values; one is consumed by the need to provide financially.

Not every person fits each of these descriptions, but a baby changes a marriage, and changes a husband and wife, individually and as a couple. The change is radical and the change is forever, because the mobile of marriage now hangs together in a whole new way.

CHILDREN REVEAL WHO WE ARE . . . NOW

As we've said before, children bring great gifts to a marriage. In addition to giving us the opportunity to experience and express a rich, rewarding new kind of love, they can be like

I love seeing how kids bring out the kid in my husband.

mirrors that reflect and reveal things about us to ourselves and to our mates. Suddenly we see a tenderness in a spouse we've never seen before! But we also come face-to-face with expressions of self-centeredness and confusing attitudes about male and female roles. Children reveal us to ourselves, reflecting back to us who we are . . . now that we are three.

Children Bring to the Surface Our Original Family Issues

Even in marriages without children, issues crop up about our parents and our original families. As psychologist Joyce Brothers claims, "When we marry someone, we marry everything that person brings from childhood."[5] But when we become parents, we begin to look at the ways in which we were parented with a new scrutiny. The truth is, how we were parented will affect who we are and how we parent. The family we grew up in will influence the family we're growing. This reality becomes clearest when children come into the marriage and suddenly you and your spouse must decide how to discipline, make and save money, and divide up the daily duties.

We don't even realize how many childhood memories we've stashed into our heads . . . until we become parents. Then they begin to flash across our minds. For instance, one day, as the new dad diapers the baby, he realizes he never saw his father do such a chore. Or, you watch your only child toddling about the house and remember how perfect life was for you as an only child—but your spouse confesses that he considers your "only child" childhood as incomplete because of the memories of his five siblings. Or, growing up in a single-parent home, you never saw your parents in partnership and, consequently, you find yourself bucking against sharing any of the load. It seems more familiar to do it all on your own.

The Bible tells us to leave our father and mother and to cleave to a mate. For some, the dependence upon and emotional attachment to a family or parents makes leaving and cleaving difficult. Author Kenneth Chafin addresses the challenge:

> . . . the decision to get married will place you in a different kind of relationship, a relationship in which the commitment to the new family created by the marriage takes precedence over the relationship with parents. This can be extremely painful for parents who do not know how to turn loose of their children. But when the break is made and the parental relationship is reestablished on more mature bases there are rich rewards for all involved.[6]

But the bridge between the families of origin and the family of now is crossed with careful and intentional effort as we define what's worth bringing across that bridge from the past to the present. Which values are worth keeping? How can differing traditions be integrated? What wounds remain from the imperfect parenting we received, and how can they be healed so they don't affect our parenting?

Issues concerning our family of origin continue throughout the lifetime of raising our children as the various ages and stages they go through continue to reveal unresolved issues from our own upbringing. In this way, children reveal us to ourselves at deeper and deeper levels.

I cannot expect my husband to meet all my needs.

Children Challenge and Clarify Our Views About Gender and Roles

"My mom always made a big meal, like pot roast and homemade pie, and the whole family ate together at noon on Sundays."

"Well, my mom took Sundays off, and we fended for ourselves. But my dad washed the dishes after *every* meal all the rest of the time."

"My dad didn't ever help in the kitchen! He sat on the couch and watched television and we kids couldn't bother him!"

Sound familiar? Most of us rarely recognize the real issues beneath these spats. But when kids come into the marriage mobile, they force husband and wife to look at gender differences, the assumptions they made, and roles they took for granted. Whether it's who cooks dinner or who doses out the discipline or who takes the

My wife has expectations of me that are unrealistic. Some of her needs can only be met by God and other women.

kids to the doctor or who mows the lawn or who pays the bills, children force couples to reconsider who does what in a marriage and why.

Gender differences, whether physiological, emotional, or otherwise, are reflected in how we relate to each other and to our world. Add to that traditional and biblical interpretations of how the two genders should relate and interact in life. Further complicating the issues are memories of how things were done when we were growing up. But rather than stereotyping the differences or bashing them, we're wise to identify them in our own marriage relationship and respect them.

Let's look at a typical issue.

Consider the question, "Who gets up in the middle of the night to help a crying child?" You may say, "The mother, of course." Okay, now answer this question: "Why?" Perhaps she's the one who meets the need because the baby is breast-feeding and she has the food. Maybe by choice she has assumed these responsibilities at home and is able to sleep later in the morning while her husband must rise early for work outside the home. Then the answer makes sense.

My husband understands that I am different, but he doesn't really understand our differences.

But what if the child is five and is having a bad dream and the mom is working from a home office and has a conference call scheduled for 7:30 the next morning? What then?

There are no magic answers or formulas based on gender or role or biblical interpretation. Most marriage counselors diagnose gender role struggles as issues of power—harmony is formed when decisions are made that simply meet the needs of spouses and children without arguments about rights and equality, offering instead a response of service to each other, day in and day out.

Author, wife, and mother Ruth Senter addresses the potential conflict about gender roles with this question: "Whatever happened to the notion that marriage is a joint union of shared energy, shared surrendering up for the sake of another? . . . Marriage is a coming together in a joyful union of mutual surrender."[7] Writer Danielle Crittenden, in an article entitled "The Argument Against Equal Marriage," assesses the assumptions of modern marriages in which couples are so preoccupied with the balance of power that many are unable or unwilling to make commonplace accommodations to married life.

> But it may be that in order for modern women to have the marriages we want, they may have to stop being so preoccupied with our identities, and instead develop an appreciation for the mutual, if differing, contributions we make to a marriage as men and women. Maybe what we should expect from our marriages is not so much an equality in kind but an equality in spirit. We want our husbands to love and respect us, to see us as their equal in all aspects of the mind and soul, but that doesn't mean we have to do exactly the same things in our day-to-day lives or occupy identical roles. We must also understand that family has never been about promotion of rights but about the surrender of them—by both the man *and* the woman. A wife and husband give up their sexual freedom, their financial freedom, their right to pursue happiness entirely on their own terms the moment they leave the altar. No matter what may come of their marriage, they have tied their identities—and fates—together. Through the act of having children, they seal them.[8]

Children Broaden Our Personalities

A schedule-oriented woman who delights in order and predictability and control usually discovers the need to be more flexible when she has a child. A stern, demanding man might soften with the presence of a newborn in his life. Children broaden the narrowness of our viewpoints, teach us about self-sacrifice, and stretch us to develop new aspects of our personalities.

Raising children tells you new things about your spouse as well as about yourself. As your husband carefully sterilizes the pacifier, you marvel at such attention from this man who never seems to notice his dirty underwear in the bedroom corner. She reads a bedtime story with great pathos, and you smile at the dramatic expression escaping from her typically shy personality. Suddenly you realize: "Oh my gosh—I married you!"

REDISCOVER YOUR RELATIONSHIP

Okay. So you're different from who you used to be. And so is your spouse. And so are the two of you together. All these differences cause the imbalance in your marriage mobile. So what's next? How do you begin to adjust and regain a new sense of balance? As you apply the following four principles to your new identities, you will rediscover a new depth and balance in your relationship.

> *Trying to think like my wife and see life from her perspective helps me meet the needs of our marriage.*

Separate But Together Yields Interdependence

There are two components that combine to make up the concept of interdependence in marriage. They are *separate* . . . and . . . *together.* Oddly, both concepts are contained in the meaning of the word *cleave.* It means "split apart," as a meat cleaver splits apart a piece of meat. But it also means "join together," as God directs couples who are getting married. This is how author Ed Wheat describes cleaving:

> To cling to or adhere to, abide fast, cleave fast together, follow close and hard after, be joined together, keep fast . . . to cement together, to stick like glue—or be welded together so that the two cannot be separated without damage to both.[9]

First, let's consider the "togetherness" part of the word. After all, that's what makes marriage different from singleness, right? Sharing common interests, hanging out, renting an apartment or buying a home and furnishing it, romance, companionship, partnering for life—these elements make up the togetherness of marriage. Before marrying, you kept your own schedule and informed no one (except maybe your parents once a week or so) of your daily agenda. After marriage, especially with children, your schedule becomes your mate's and you share every detail necessary to make things work in the life of your family. Togetherness seals you in union where you think and act with others in mind. In fact, togetherness is necessary for a couple's survival in a marriage with children.

I need small breaks to be by myself, to be an individual, to find out who I am and who I want to become.

— ✳ —

I try not to limit my husband's time with his golfing friends unless we just aren't seeing each other.

— ✳ —

Caring for "dependents" breeds an increased dependency on each other.

Separateness, the other component of interdependence, is a bit more surprising, because it's so easy to forget, especially after kids come! Separateness is the realization and enactment of the fact that husband and wife are not extensions of each other. Neither are they extensions of their children or their children extensions of them. Each spouse is an individual, with thoughts, needs, and a personality all to themselves. In some ways husband and wife are alike, but in other ways they are different. This separateness is lived out emotionally and physically. No couple should be together twenty-four hours every day. Understanding and allowing for such physical and emotional separation is vital to the marriage.

When togetherness and separateness unite, they yield interdependence. This new state is characterized by an understanding of each person's uniqueness and individuality, yet the desire to unite and interweave these two separate lives into one unit. One marriage therapist labels this aspect of marriage *autonomy* and defines it as "separateness and a healthy degree of independence—the ability to stand on one's own two feet and function well in the world. In the healthiest marriages, each partner has a clear and distinct sense of self, and the inevitable conflicts are negotiated effectively."[10]

The symbol of this "separate but togetherness" is often marked in the lighting of a unity candle in a wedding ceremony.

Usually there are three candles. The two outside ones, representing the bride and groom, are lighted, sometimes by the bride's and groom's parents. The center one is unlighted until the couple is pronounced husband and wife. Then they each take the outside candles and together they light the single center candle, blowing out the outside candles before placing them back in their holders. Pastor and author Kenneth Chafin describes his reaction to watching this part of the ceremony:

> Then something happened I was not really prepared for. Each took his/her lighted candle and blew it out. I wanted to shout, "No." In a sense each was saying now that this new relationship was formed they no longer existed as individuals, it seemed to me. That's not so. All three exist, the bride, the groom, and the marriage.

> Today, when a couple asks me to perform their wedding and want to use the unity candle, I agree on one condition. I ask them to please not blow out their candle and to please continue to grow and develop as individuals because the middle candle, the marriage, depends on it.[11]

The three burning candles symbolize this healthy "separate but together" perspective.

Respect

As you rediscover your relationship, respect will play a vital role. A stay-at-home mom may ask, "How can I get my husband to believe that I'm busy at home all day?" A husband might complain, "She acts like my efforts with the baby aren't as important as hers. Is it because I didn't *labor* to bring our child into the world?" Both remark, "How can we be more unified in our discipline? We seem to undo each other's efforts." Or, "How can we respect each

The added demands of having children has given us a more concrete understanding of how we can bless each other by being each other's "completer" as we raise our children together.

other's individual needs, apart from our marriage and parenting roles?"

Years ago, W. B. Yeats remarked, "I have spread my dreams under your feet; Tread softly because you tread on my dreams." His words describe the challenge before us as husband and wife. In the tender process of redefining ourselves with the addition of a child to a marriage, we have to respect inevitable differences. Differences from ourselves. Differences from our expectations. Even differences from our dreams.

Ministers in wedding ceremonies sometimes direct a message to the bride and groom about this kind of respect. "Lindsay," the minister might say to the bride, "imagine getting to heaven at the end of your life. Jesus might ask you ... *Is your husband more of the person I created him to be because he lived with you?* I hope you will be able to answer yes." Then the minister asks the groom the same question.

> *I put my children's needs first because they are dependent upon me; my husband is not.*

To check your progress in this earthly endeavor ask yourself these questions: "Am I helping my spouse to reach his/her God-given potential?" "Is my spouse better because I'm in his/her life?" "How am I encouraging my spouse's uniqueness through our marriage?"

Acceptance

Closely tied to respect is acceptance. Not only do we need to respect and honor our spouse for who they are separate from us, we also need to reach a place of accepting them. Acceptance is a lifelong struggle in a marriage with children. Three facets make up the challenge of accepting your spouse.

First, his way versus her way. *Different* doesn't mean wrong, and *different* doesn't mean better. A wife tells the story of her husband dressing their nine-month-old daughter for the day, buttoning up her outfit in the back. When he brought the baby to her for a good morning hug, the wife giggled and said,

"You've got that on wrong. It's backwards! I always button it up the front!"

Puzzled, the dad checked inside the neckline to find the tag, appropriately sewn by the buttons and in the "back." With chagrin, the wife realized she'd been buttoning up her daughter's outfit backwards. But did it matter? The outfit actually looked fine either way. *Different* doesn't mean *wrong*.

We're very different, my husband and me, and having children gives us a common passion (besides the obvious one).

Singer Annie Chapman tells of the time she left their two-week-old son with her husband—with explicit instructions about feeding him and changing his diapers. She returned three hours later to find the baby wet and dirty. "Steve is a terrific father," she concluded, "but he's still a lousy mother. He's not aware of some of the details I feel are important, like brushing teeth and changing underwear. But when it comes to having a good time with the kids and making them feel special, Steve can't be beat."[13]

Sometimes, in order to accept our spouse's way of doing things, we have to give up our own rigid agendas or attitudes. Insistence that one way is right and one way is wrong turns *his* way versus *her* way into a disagreement, especially when the issues are child-related. Just as couples learned early in marriage that there are several ways to squeeze the toothpaste and hang wallpaper, so they learn in parenting that *different* doesn't necessarily mean better (or worse!).

Second, friends versus foes. It's easy in marriage to want to *change* our spouses. Maybe marriage ought to resemble friendships in this matter. Isn't a friend someone who is happy to see you and has no agenda to change you? Someone who accepts who you are and walks beside you? Shouldn't a spouse be at least a friend? Determine to accept and love your spouse, instead of always trying to change that person into someone else.

Third, warts and all. Acceptance comes easiest when we see our spouse as he or she is—imperfect, just like us—and choose to love him or her, warts and all, imperfections and irritations included. Writers Jim and Jeri White explain, "Acceptance begins with the belief that God has given us someone of value as our marriage partner, and with an attitude, therefore, of being pleased with our mate even though this person isn't perfect."[14]

While acceptance means wholly embracing our mate, it doesn't mean permanently resigning ourselves to the parts that are destructive to our relationship. When we see selfishness, we can accept it but not give in to it. When we observe a difference in direction of our spouse's heart from ours, we can understand it without relinquishing our heart to it as well.

Accepting the imperfection of a spouse means embracing the possibility of no change while still praying for progress. One mom, who was disappointed in the lack of spiritual leadership in her husband, criticized and cajoled him to attend church with her and the children. She met with resistance, and finally changed her tactics on this advice from a friend: "Don't talk to your mate about God," her friend advised. "Talk to God about your mate." Another woman who kept trying to change her husband decided to stop expecting her husband to change and began asking God to change her.

Learning to accept a spouse, in spite of differences, in spite of imperfections, builds a stronger marriage, especially through transitions of life.

Freedom

There is one more gift we give our mate that provides interdependence and underlines our commitment to his or her growing identity. This gift is freedom, and it requires allowing your spouse to be the best he or she can be, in whatever form that takes.

One woman provides freedom for her husband by decreeing her home a "no smothering zone." Utilizing the tools of trust, acceptance, encouragement, and involvement, she is devoted to making their home a haven of freedom from the criticism and pressure to change.

> *My wife gives me the confidence to be the person I am.*
>
> — x* —
>
> *I'd like to help my wife feel important and needed outside her role as a mother.*

Another woman recognizes the gift of unconditional freedom her husband offers to her. She writes, "My husband understands me. He accepts that, try as I might, some irritating things about me aren't going to change because they're near-chemical components of my makeup. Home is where, when I go there, he takes me in every time."[15]

This poem, entitled *A Growing Love*, by Ulrich Schaffer, expresses freedom found in the interdependence of a couple:

> Your freedom
> Is always tied in with mine
> I can let you go free fully
> If I am being let go by you
> My freedom liberates you
> Which liberates me
> Which liberates you
> Etc.
> Etc.
> Etc.
> It can be an upward
> Or a downward spiral
> I can choose
> You can choose
> We can choose.[16]

Our children depend on us for every-thing, so it's important we learn to depend on each other.

Freedom in marriage encourages the growth that keeps the relationship vital through the years.

CONCLUSION

Children change a couple's identities, individually and to-gether. As husband and wife become mom and dad, they take on new roles and responsibilities and emotions that forever change who they are. Sometimes one changes more than the other, and nudges the other toward change. It's been said that change is difficult, and that "people change when the pain of re-maining the same becomes greater than the pain of changing."[17]

As a couple faces the reality of change, separately and to-gether, they learn to recognize and accept these changes and re-discover their relationship in the middle of their new roles. They seek a healthy interdependence as they continue to weave their lives together and strengthen the bonds that unite them.

MOBILIZER #1: LIGHTEN UP

The Rules

1. The FEMALE always makes the Rules.

2. The Rules are subject to change at anytime without prior notification.

3. No MALE can possibly know all the Rules.

4. If the FEMALE suspects the MALE knows the Rules, she must immediately change some or all of the Rules.

5. The FEMALE is never wrong.

6. If the FEMALE is wrong it is because of a Flagrant Misunderstanding that was a direct result of something the MALE did or said.

7. If Rule #6 applies, the MALE must apologize immediately for causing the misunderstanding.

8. The FEMALE can change her mind at any time.

9. The MALE must never change his mind without the Express Consent of the FEMALE.

10. The FEMALE has every right to be angry and upset at any time.

11. The MALE must remain calm at all times unless the FEMALE wants him to be angry and upset.

12. If the FEMALE has PMS, all Rules are Null and Void.18

Rules Guys Wished Girls Knew

1.   If you think you're fat, you probably are. Please don't ask us.
2.   Learn to work the toilet seat; if it's up, put it down.
3.   Shopping is not a sport.
4.   Anything you wear is fine. Really.
5.   Ask for what you want. Subtle hints don't work.
6.   A headache that lasts for seventeen days is a problem. See a doctor.
7.   Anything we said six or eight months ago is inadmissible in an argument.
8.   You can either ask us to do something OR tell us how you want it done—not both.

MOBILIZER #2: LOVE GROWS AND CHANGES US

Love Grows Us

I love you,
Not only for what you are,
But for what I am
When I am with you.
I love you,
Not only for what
You have made of yourself,
But for what
You are making of me.

ROY CROFT[19]

MOBILIZER #3: MARRIAGE, MASCULINITY, AND FEMININITY

One woman's viewpoint:

For the first years of my marriage, I was under the tragic misperception that my husband was the only legitimate source of all good things in my life. I looked to him to fulfill all my needs for friendship, for romance, for direction in decision making, and for emotional support when I was feeling blue. . . .

As if this weren't enough of a burden for him to carry, I began looking to him for my sense of feminine confidence. His words, his responses to me, his actions toward me became my sole source of how I perceived myself as a woman. . . .

I know too many women who make the same mistake. Somehow, we get this idea that the men in our lives are supposed to be our all in all—that somehow they are the sources of our happiness, that they have the power to fulfill all our needs. What's more, it's up to them to make us feel pretty, feminine, nurtured, pampered, fulfilled, desirable.

What are we thinking? Thank heaven our husbands don't put the same demands on us. No, men tend to get their sense of self-esteem and masculine confidence from a variety of sources: their careers, financial accomplishments, athletics, hobbies, competitive razzing with male buddies, and, yes, their wives. I'm glad I'm represented on the list; I'm also glad I do not single-handedly comprise the list. Imagine the pressure I'd live with if I knew I was the sole source of my husband's masculinity! Yet this is the burden we too often heave onto the broad but human shoulders of the men we love.[20]

MOBILIZER #4: LEAVING AND CLEAVING

There are several steps any couple can take (no matter how long they have been married) to leave home.

First, *work at establishing a peer relationship with your parents.* This isn't always easy. But genuine growth means graduating from childlike ways of responding to others (even to our parents).

Second, *take a long, honest look at your past.* Your past influences you, and your spouse sees that most acutely. You should do your best to tackle your past (see Mobilizer #5). For some, such a process may involve a skilled Christian counselor.

Third, *be careful not to equate leaving home with simply doing the opposite of what your parents say.* As adults, it does not work to do the opposite of what our parents say simply to establish our independence. In a healthy peer relationship, we should evaluate our parents' counsel to see how it squares with Scripture and common sense (and then honor their advice if we can).[21]

MOBILIZER #5: DEALING WITH YOUR PAST

Here's an exercise to help you deal with your past. Gather as many old family photos as possible. Over a long afternoon or evening, discuss why the situations in the pictures were photographed. Take note of who was always in the pictures and who was left out. What memories, patterns, or emotions emerge as you view your life through the years?

You may be uncomfortable with this exercise because it can bring to the surface feelings you have avoided for years. Perhaps you will see all over again how favored your sister was or how all the photos featured the athlete of the family, not the band member. Perhaps your father was never in the picture because he rarely took time to be with you.

Whatever the pictures reveal, the truth of John 8:32 needs to be your guide: "You will know the truth, and the truth will set you free." For those with a background full of hurt, it is only by honestly facing their past that they will ever be free from its control.[22]

MOBILIZER #6: HOW WELL
DO YOU KNOW YOUR SPOUSE?

How much do you know about your spouse? Here are some questions about your spouse that will test your knowledge. Answer the questions separately and compare notes afterward.

1. Where was I born?
2. What was one of my greatest achievements as a child?
3. What was one of my favorite activities when I was a child?
4. If we went to a restaurant for dinner, what would I be most likely to order?
5. Who is my favorite recording artist?
6. What is my favorite book? TV program?
7. What one thing do you do that annoys me most?
8. If I had tomorrow totally free, what would I like to do most?
9. What do I fear the most?
10. What would I like to be doing five years from now? Ten years from now?

MOBILIZER #7: POSTPARTUM BLUES ARE REAL

Characterized by weepiness, anxiety, and lack of motivation, the baby blues affect up to seventy-five percent of new moms within the first ten days after delivery. Only about ten percent of moms experience more serious postpartum depression (PPD). Unfortunately, little is known about the cause of PPD, although the dramatic shifting of a new mom's hormones is a suspected culprit. Some symptoms that may indicate PPD are:

- Not being able to get out of bed due to fatigue
- Overconcern for the baby, lack of interest in the baby, or fear of being alone with the baby
- Inability to sleep
- A rise or fall in appetite
- Exaggerated mood swings
- Uncontrollable crying (past a couple of weeks after delivery)

Treatment for the condition usually includes changes in diet, the addition of vitamins, and counseling.

Another major contributor to PPD is the notion that new moms should be able to do it all: take care of the new baby (and other siblings), do the laundry, cook, and entertain visitors. If you have problems getting things done, get help. Motherhood is a big transition, and you shouldn't expect to do it all alone.

Questions to Ask Each Other

- How has being a parent changed us as individuals?
- How has parenting changed us as a couple?
- What did our parents do that we'd like to repeat in our marriage? In our parenting?
- What did our parents do that we'd like to *not* repeat in our marriage? In our parenting?
- What do we like to do together?
- What do each of us like to do individually?
- How can we respect each other's individuality?
- How do we depend on each other?

Recommended Reading

Boundaries, Henry Cloud and John Townsend
Getting the Love You Want: A Guide for Couples, Harville
 Hendrix
Let Me Ask You This, Chap and Dee Clark
Maximum Marriage, Tim Timmons
Men Are from Mars, Women Are from Venus, John Gray
The Two Sides of Love, Gary Smalley and John Trent
What Husbands Wish Their Wives Knew About Men, Patrick M.
 Morley
Women Are Always Right and Men Are Never Wrong, Joey
 O'Connor

Four

Intimacy

REESTABLISHING YOUR INTIMACY

Are we just roommates?

Eric paid the airport shuttle driver, then bounded up the front steps.

"I'm home!" he shouted as he dumped his suitcase in the hall and went in search of his family: his wife, to be specific.

"Kristen?" A complete tour of their usual hangouts in the house produced nothing but emptiness and silence. He opened the screen door in the kitchen and looked outside, straining for sounds of the kids playing on the swings in the side yard. Nothing.

Her car was in the drive, but Kristen wasn't around. Rats. He'd missed her this past week while on the road with his job. The kids too. Even though their lives turned his into bedlam, he loved the wide-armed welcome offered by Josh (age three) and Emily (almost eighteen months) when he came through the door each evening.

Just then, Eric heard them burst through the garage door.

"I wanted to stay longer at the park, Mommy," Josh whined.

"Emily, no!" Kristen scolded. "Remember, Mommy doesn't want you to dump the sand out of your shoes inside!"

"Hey, guys! I'm home!" Eric announced.

"Daddy!" the children shouted as they toddled towards him. Kristen smiled. "Hi, honey. You're home early . . . and just in time. I think I'm running out of steam here!"

Eric gathered the kids in his arms and leaned to give his wife a kiss with an extra little nibble on her lower lip, his intimate signal to her that he wanted more than a kiss. She patted his cheek. From that point on, the evening proceeded much as usual. Dinner was chaotic with conversation punctuated by interruptions and cranky tempers. Then bathtime. Storytime. Bedtime. Drink-of-water-time. Then bedtime again. At last, silence, which meant alone time for Eric and Kristen.

Eric unpacked his suitcase and then turned to find Kristen on the phone with her mom. He sighed. He really wanted her full attention. After all, it had been over two weeks since they'd made love. Maybe if he got into bed, she would join him, he decided, so he climbed into bed and picked up his computer magazine.

A few minutes later, Kristen hung up the phone and saw Eric reading. She sighed. She needed to talk. He'd been gone so long, and they were trying to cut back on their phone bill so he'd only called twice this week. Frustrated by his lack of attention, Kristen headed for the bathroom, changed into her familiar T-shirt jammies, and then crawled into bed next to her husband, who by now had nodded off.

Her movement must have awakened him, because he stirred and reached for Kristen, offering the warmth of ready-to-go affection. But instead of embracing his overture, Kristen stiffened and nudged him away. More physical giving out tonight? No way. She felt like she was running on empty after a long week with the children, and she needed refilling. She needed words, not sex.

Confused by her rebuff, Eric sat up and looked at her. "What's the matter? I've been gone all week and it's been so long. Didn't you miss me?"

WHAT INTIMACY ISN'T AND WHAT IT IS

You can vaguely remember it. That passion that was desire that translated into *action!* It arose from a tingly conviction that you *loved* your spouse and your spouse *loved* you! You'd look into each other's eyes and *know* what the other was thinking. You couldn't keep your hands off each other. You *always* wanted to kiss. You could talk for *hours* and never tire. What happened to those long ago and far away days? What happened to intimacy?

Intimacy is an important part of the bond that ties a married couple together, but establishing and maintaining intimacy isn't easy. "Living intimately with another human being is the greatest challenge in the world."[1] So say Bill and Lynne Hybels in their book about marriage, *Fit to Be Tied*. And most of us agree. But sometimes we get romance and intimacy confused. Let's look at the meaning of intimacy.

Intimacy Means "Into-Me-See"

Perhaps we best understand what intimacy is by addressing what it isn't. Intimacy isn't just romance or sex. It's not roses and chocolates and moonlight cruises. Neither is it reading minds and anticipating needs. While these ingredients help create an environment where intimacy can grow, none of them guarantee it.

You could say that intimacy is "into-me-see."[2] The Latin word for *inner* or *innermost* is *intimus*. From this root comes our word *intimate*. Webster defines *intimate* as "that which characterizes one's deepest nature, personal."

It's hard to feel like being physically intimate when I don't feel like we are emotionally and intellectually intimate.

— ✗ —

We need more shared or mutual interests or hobbies.

— ✗ —

We need short vacations without the kids.

Yes, intimacy is "into-me-see." It's caring enough to take the time and make the effort to understand the soul and heart of another person—and to communicate this understanding back. In his book *The Secrets of a Lasting Marriage,* H. Norman Wright identifies several different dimensions of intimacy that combine to build intimate relationships:

> *Emotional intimacy:* a feeling of closeness that comes from sharing all emotions, both pain and joy, and communicates mutual caring support to both partners.
>
> *Social intimacy:* having mutual friends to play with and talk with, rather than socializing separately.
>
> *Intellectual intimacy:* sharing and stimulating each other's level of knowledge.
>
> *Recreational intimacy:* enjoying the same interests and activities.
>
> *Sexual intimacy:* finding mutually enjoyable physical acts of love that meet each other's needs.[3]

We're trying to be open and honest with each other and share our feelings, both positive and negative, about being a wife, husband, mommy, and daddy.

— *x** —

My husband is uncomfortable talking about emotions and wants to move quickly to solutions.

Intimacy in Marriage

Several ingredients help us apply the concept of intimacy to marriage. Each of these ingredients of intimacy allow partners to feel known at many different levels in many different ways.

Intimacy begins with vulnerability. Marriage therapist John T. Gossett suggests that intimacy has to do with vulnerability: "You are intimate if each of you can say anything, no matter how silly or frightened or immature or helpless it makes you look, and the other person will treat it with respect, not use it against you."[4] Being vulnerable carries with it the ingredient of risk. When we open ourselves up to each other, we are risking ridicule and pain.

Intimacy grows with shared history. Over time, we grow more intimate as we share more and more feelings and more and more of our life experiences. James Dobson suggests, "When two people love each other deeply and are committed for life, they have usually developed a great volume of understandings between

> *When we disagree, we remind each other that we're on the same team.*
>
> — ⚜ —
>
> *My wife reminds me of romantic times in our past and points out the romantic things I do.*

them that would be considered insignificant to anyone else. They share countless private memories unknown to the rest of the world. That is in large measure where their sense of specialness to one another originates."[5]

Intimacy is expressed sexually in marriage. Unique to the marriage relationship is the expression of intimacy through sexual interaction. "Sexual intimacy," writes Karen Scalf Linamen, "is, indeed, the single dynamic that makes a marriage something more than a lifetime business partnership or a co-op between roommates."[6] "Into-me-see" love is uniquely expressed in marriage through sexual union.

> *I would like my wife to be insanely filled with lust about once a week.*

Intimacy builds on commitment and identity. As we discussed in previous chapters, commitment gives a couple the security and assurance of their love, and healthy identity means knowing yourself and feeling comfortable about being yourself, which gives a person a great sense of freedom. "You cannot have intimacy out of a false self," write Brent Curtis and John Eldredge in *The Sacred Romance.*[7]

Intimacy makes marriage comfortable. As married love passes through life's seasons, it becomes "comfortable." One mother of young children penned this poem to her husband to express this quality.

Comfortable Love

There's a thing I call comfortable love.
It's not new or shiny or flashy.
It's more like a bear with the fur loved off,
all comfy, cozy, and warm.
It's a love that's passed the test of time,
much deeper than new love could possibly be.
This love is filled with history,
passion through joys and despair.
This love produces strength and security,
like a baby blanket from younger days.
Comfortable love is what I share with you,
growing more valuable, more precious,
more comfortable each day.[8]

The opposite sex never understands the opposite sex.

HOW CHILDREN CHANGE INTIMACY

Here's the typical cycle of most marriages, according to Becky Freeman in *Marriage 911:*

Baby arrives. Man watches lover turn into mother. Man misses wife. Woman feels pulled in two. Baby drains energy needed for couple to do anything about it. Just when life gets under control, the home pregnancy test turns blue again.[9]

No doubt about it, children change intimacy in marriage in conflicting ways. They both deepen and diminish it. We all know their mere presence often snuffs out the fire. But before we look at the challenges children pose to intimacy, let's look first at the benefits they bring.

Children Deepen Intimacy

From the moment we receive the news that we're having a baby, the definition of love takes on new meaning. Suddenly sex is more than a delightful pastime of bliss and mutual joy. It is an act with a *creative purpose,* and we are awed that we are participating in the miracle of forming a new life. Then, after the child is born, we are amazed that "every cell of this child is made up of us. Every propensity is the result of our combined essence. There is something about knowing all this that sends romantic shivers down our spines."[10]

And then comes the intimacy of sharing the joint project of being partners in parenting! Unbelievable! Where we once combined efforts to select china patterns or a sofa or even a car, now our efforts center on a child—a life—a human being who has come from us and will go out into the world one day as an inde-

Having children has taken our relationship to a new level—it has matured our relationship.

pendent being, carrying our influence into the next generation. This awesome responsibility bonds us together like nothing else, as we turn to each other for strength and hope.

With the forming of and responsibility for new life, a couple's intimacy deepens into something previously unimagined.

Children Also Diminish Intimacy

All marriages struggle to retain, grow, and enjoy marital intimacy. In fact, Dennis Rainey believes that the number one problem confronting married couples today is a lack of intimacy or "husbands excluding wives and wives excluding husbands."[12] But the threat children bring to marital intimacy is unique.

I'm tired and have a hard time feeling sexual.

— x* —

I need my husband's help with
putting the children to bed so we can be together.

— x* —

I don't always like sharing my wife's attention with our two little boys.

One mom put it this way,

> Having a baby changed everything. My husband and I continued to go through the motions of our lives, paying bills, answering phone calls, fixing dinner, but there seemed to be no world outside of our home, no sound other than the cooing or crying of our son. My husband and I would smile vaguely at each other over dinner and quickly turn our attention back to the perfect little body asleep in my arms. Our baby was our only passion. Marriage was an afterthought.[13]

In our marriage mobiles, children blow a strong wind on the aspect of intimacy. Keep reading and see if you've experienced any of these gales in your relationship.

Exhaustion. Male or female, parents of young children are often too tired to be intimate. It takes too much effort at the end of an already jam-packed day. First we're up early to feed a baby or get off to work—or both. Then we face all the other tasks of life (like shopping, cleaning, bill-paying, and personal hygiene) *in addition* to the responsibilities of parenting. By the time mom nurses the baby and all the little ones are nighty-night, her body is done for the day. As humorist Liz Curtis Higgs says, wives want to tell our husbands that "this body can only do one thing at a time!"

Time. Sometimes it's the second child that sends our marriage mobile spinning out of control. We grow accustomed to one baby and still find time for each other. But with the second, and the development of the first to the point where he or she needs *constant* supervision, there's not a morsel of time left over for anything else. One mother claimed it was the third child that did them in. "It was when we had to switch from a man-to-man defense to a zone defense. That's when we realized we had no time left for each other."

Interruptions. Children *are* interruptions. They interrupt our conversations, our sleep, and our romantic moods. We all know the scene. The children are in bed. The fire is crackling, candles flickering. The afghan is cozying you together as you cuddle, and the mood is growing. Suddenly you look up to see a footie-jammie-clad toddler pulling at his ear and whimpering, "I don't feel good!"

Or there's the story of the couple who made it all the way to their bedroom. "Assuming our kids were sound asleep, we were totally caught up in the romance of the moment, when a little voice at the side of our bed said, 'Daddy, can I ride next?'"[14]

One story like that, and even the fear of interruptions blows the whole idea of intimacy with children in the house.

> *I've missed our spontaneity. Having children has made us plan everything to the nth detail.*

Reality. Then there's the reality that bursts the bubble of our idealistic expectations. We thought marriage would be filled with consistently sensitive, loving awareness of each other, and instead it's soured with the reality of meeting incessant needs of children. No wonder most couples experience a growing numbness toward each other. Here's how one mom reports her adjustment:

> There's nothing like a baby to bring a pair of romantic dreamers down to earth. With three children I feel so firmly planted I could be a shrub, and my dream has become ownership of a station wagon. Now, even when we find a rare moment together, uninterrupted by a child demanding raisins, or a baby wanting to be fed, or a ringing phone, what we find ourselves talking about is (as once it was each other) the children.

She goes on to describe a subject which invades many young marriages: travel and absence.

> Where once a night apart seemed almost physically painful, now my husband's job takes him away one week out of every two and, lately, every week, with two-day visits home on weekends. It's not a rhythm any of us would have chosen, and I hope some day it changes, but for now we're getting by.[15]

Other loves. It's funny how the "reality checks" in marriage can send us reeling back to fantasize about previous relationships and prior loves. In the early days of parenthood, it is common for both men and women to confess dreaming of visits from old boyfriends and girlfriends. It's as if we're wondering about what might have been and comparing it to what is.

One woman revealed her dream this way,

> Last night I had a dream about a high-school boyfriend who came back into my life and swept me off my feet. That nostalgic rush of young-love feelings swept over me: the elevated pulse, the longing to be touched, the kinds of desires that often get buried in the barrage of daily details and children's needs and married love.

> My dream progressed excitingly, to the point that I was to marry this high-school flame. And then I experienced another familiar emotion—that aching longing I used to feel as a child when I was about to go off on my own, to camp or a long weekend away from home—a homesickness for my security.

> I wailed in my dream, and my wailing must have awakened me . . . to find my husband lying beside me, snoring. Somehow I was thankful.

While the memory or temptation of other loves occurs through all seasons of marriage, it uniquely rears its head in the season of marriage with young children when couples are adjusting to the reality of their lifemate choices at deeper and deeper levels.

Life pain. No one in marriage can be prepared for the unwelcome guest of life pain. When a tragedy or crisis arrives uninvited on the doorstep of a home, no

I want my wife to believe in me.

one wants to open the door to let it in. Yet, in it comes anyway. The death of a parent or a child. The loss of a job, or a transition to a new one, or a transfer to a new city. An illness. Depression. The processing of issues from long ago and far away. All these events can be part of life at any age, but they seem uniquely disruptive to the life of a young family, still new at dealing with the reality that life rarely turns out as you expected.

And yet, such challenges often bring the opportunity for new vulnerability and honesty, and therefore, a deeper intimacy can grow out of the painful situation. We find ourselves much like a woman who struggled to know how to comfort her husband after the sudden loss of his best friend at age thirty-three. "Here was a man with whom I had shared three children, a home, and a life for twelve years. And yet we didn't know each other well enough to cry together. Our marriage had never taken either of us to this level before. It had always been like a business, with each of us carrying out our individual roles. He was the provider, and I was the nurturer who could handle anything. Not to handle it was perceived as a weakness."

She describes passing by the bedroom door and seeing him sitting on the bed, alone in his guilt. She pauses and then walks in and sits down beside him. They begin to share memories about this friend, and finally, they cry together. Later she reflects, "Throughout our years together, we had built up a history and a closeness so subtle even we didn't know it was there. On that evening, we admitted we couldn't handle life alone. We needed each other."[16]

It seems the wild winds wail against the concept of intimacy in these early years of marriage with kids. For many couples, the marriage mobile swings crazily, searching for enough stillness to

I want my wife to be bold and say what she needs to say.

recover, to reestablish the intimacy it once knew. And yet, just as we've learned that our identities change with children in marriage, our intimacy must adjust as well. We're not the same people we were when we got married. We have changed. Our intimacy must change as well.

WITHSTANDING THE WILD WINDS

Several clear tracks can be taken to reestablish intimacy in your marriage mobile. Some are so obviously simple you'll be tempted to laugh them off with "Right—so what?" Perhaps that's the point. Most of us make our lives far too complicated. We desperately long to create the kind of marriage that will provide a secure spot for our children to grow and mature. The truth is, these simple techniques have worked for other couples with children, and will help you reestablish intimacy if you try them.

Rest

Very obvious, right? Then why don't we do more resting? Somehow we all buy into the myth that we have to do it *all;* do it all *right now*, and do it all *right*, right now. The concept of "fast-tracking" has infiltrated every aspect of human existence in the Western world. Even families.

When we disagree, we take turns describing our feelings on the issue, uninterrupted, so we both feel heard. Then we start to compromise.

Rabbi Naomi Levy challenges us to take a tip from the Old Testament. "Imagine what it might feel like to take a day out of each week and spend it in pure restfulness; not a day to get our errands done or to go out to the movies or the mall, but a day when we restore our souls."[17]

It sounds good, but we struggle with the application. Perhaps we make too big a deal of our resting, assuming it means "getting away from it all." We think we have to spend money or go out of town or somewhere away from home to rest.

Or it might be that we have a hard time resting because we don't see the value in it. We value *doing*, not *being*; producing, not resting. It's a matter of priorities and perspective. As Rabbi Levy says, "When we rest, we don't *miss out* on life, we learn to *appreciate* life."[18]

Try taking Sundays off. Go to church, and then do *nothing*. If you can't take Sundays off, schedule another day that you can rest. Be intentional. Mark it on your calendar. Nap when the kids nap. Lay in the grass and look at the clouds together. Eat finger foods off paper plates. Keep it simple. And then do the same thing next Sunday and the next. Rest replenishes our hearts and souls and enables us to have energy to nurture our marriages.

Need Each Other

In today's world, we value independence. We believe we're protecting ourselves and our mates when we distance ourselves emotionally and learn to go it alone. *I don't want to be a bother,* we think. *He needs some space. She'd rather me be strong.* Whatever words work, we delude ourselves if we think independence shows strength and maturity, and therefore is better.

Intimacy in marriage is about learning to need each other, being comfortable with that need, and communicating that need. It's about realizing, day in and day out, that it is *not* good that man or woman is alone, but that we are better off together. Though it may feel like a risk, we reestablish intimacy by being vulnerable and open, by recognizing our need for each other in a new way now that we are parents together. We are codependent in a healthy way. Luciano de Cresenzo said it well: "We are each of us angels with only one wing. And we can only fly embracing each other."[19]

Communicate

Good communication is essential in marriage, and it's often a challenge. Both husbands and wives listed communication as their number one problem area in the surveys we sent to one thousand moms and dads. Three vital actions make up intimate communication: listening, talking, and fighting fair. Let's look at them one at a time.

Listening. Pastor Mark Brewer describes two ways to listen. We can listen to respond, or we can listen to understand. Look back over your conversations with your spouse lately and ask yourself which brand you've been applying in your relationship. If you're listening to respond, you're looking for the place where you can jump in to fix or disagree or even finish off the conversation so you can get on to other things. If you're listening to understand, you're actually laying aside your own agenda for the sole purpose of getting into the heart of your mate and seeing the world the way he or she sees it.

> *I need my husband to tell me everything he wants me to know and not assume I already know it.*
>
> — ✻ —
>
> *I used to think I was always right, but now I realize my wife thinks differently than me, and I listen more fully to what she has to say.*

Talking. Intimate communication begins with listening to understand, but there is also a time to respond. As Walter Trobisch put it in his classic book, *I Loved a Girl*, "True love communicates. Love that finds no words to express itself soon dies."[20] Some of us are naturally more verbal than others, but even nontalkers

> *When we're together, I'd like to talk less about the kids and more about us.*

can learn to dig down and put their feelings into words. It may take practice, but most worthwhile things do.

Gary Smalley and John Trent offer help for the verbally challenged in their book *The Language of Love*. In this book they describe the technique of using word pictures to unlock the gateway to intimacy. "An emotional word picture is a communication tool that uses a story or object to activate simultaneously the *emotions* and *intellect* of a person. In so doing, it causes the listener to *experience* our words, not just hear them."[21]

For instance, you might want your husband's help on a Saturday afternoon as you get ready to have people over for dinner, but he's watching a football game and tells you that he will help you later. You finally get his attention by saying, "I feel like I'm in the fourth quarter here in the kitchen. My team's behind. It's fourth down with nine yards to go and not much time on the clock. I'm stressed because I'm about to lose this game." Voila! He understands your anxiety because you've wrapped your challenge in a word picture he understands.

Fighting fair. No marriage is conflict free. Clinical psychologist Clifford Notarius, who specializes in marital therapy, claims that "it's not the differences in a marriage that cause problems but how a couple handles the differences."[22]

How do you and your spouse handle conflict? Too often conflicts are the results of little things that have grown into big things and suddenly that big thing encompasses the whole past, present, and future. Accusations include sweeping generalizations like "You *always* ..." or "you *never*...." Common

> *I don't want my husband to win the argument; I want him to understand my feelings.*
>
> — ❊ —
>
> *First we dance around our disagreements, trying to avoid them; then we talk them out.*
>
> — ❊ —
>
> *Too often we fight until one gives in.*

advice is to stay focused on the original issue and avoid saying anything you'll both regret later.

Les and Leslie Parrott offer a few more tips for handling the ticklish spots of conflict in intimacy:

- **Don't run from strife.** Realize that you *will* fight. When issues come up, commit to dealing with them directly.
- **Choose your battles carefully.** One of the major tasks of marriage is learning what can and should be changed and what should be overlooked.
- **Define the issue clearly.** To identify the real source of conflict, you must address the questions, "What are we really quarreling about?" and "What is the real source of our disagreement?"
- **State your feelings directly.** Try the "X, Y, Z" formula. "In situation X, when you do Y, I feel Z."
- **Rate the intensity of your feelings.** For partners who aren't verbally expressive, assigning a number on a scale of 1–10 can help translate the level of their emotions to the other.
- **Give up put-downs.** Research shows that it only takes one put-down to undo hours of kindness, so show your mate kindness by avoiding them altogether.[23]

Then, of course, there are these other common reminders:

- **Use "I" messages.** Instead of the accusation, "You always leave your clothes on the floor," try "I feel resentful when I have to pick up after you and the children."
- **Avoid generalizations.** "You always" or "you never" triggers anger and defensiveness that blocks communication.
- **Win the right battle.** Ask yourself what's most important, to be *right* or to *right* the relationship?
- **Pick the time and place to settle conflict.** Sometimes taking a time-out and agreeing to discuss the conflict later is the best plan.

Make Love

"I shared breakfast in bed with a handsome young man this morning. Trouble is, he's only twenty-nine inches long and his breakfast was me, and I'm still hungry."

This statement sums up the most common kind of intimacy for some mothers of preschoolers. The father's stories aren't much better. Obviously, at some point earlier in your life, you enjoyed making love and found time to do so. Otherwise there wouldn't be any children, and you wouldn't be reading this book! But oh, the seeming impossibility of having sex these days! Yet, as we've said, making love strengthens the bonds of intimacy and is an important part of the marriage relationship, even after children are born.

In fact, a healthy sexual relationship between parents is healthy for kids. In her book, *Pillow Talk*, Karen Scalf Linamen suggests that "the bond that is created by sexual intimacy between you and your husband does far more than enhance your relationship alone—it also enriches the lives of your children."[24] Children thrive in a home where they know mom and dad love each other.

> We have a small group of friends who get together every New Year's Eve. The first year the host suggested we be prepared to share the most unusual place we made love in the last year. I just knew my darling husband would die of shame not having anything interesting to claim, so on an unusually warm December evening we went out in the backyard on the trampoline and created a story. Mind you, I am very conservative and highly modest, but I have to say it was an exciting adventure. It's now become a yearly tradition to make a story and it certainly spices things up.

But men and women have different appetites for sex, especially after children are born, and bringing balance back to this part of your marriage requires good communication, flexibility, and a commitment to work at sexual intimacy together. In the opening story, both Eric and Kristen wanted intimacy, but Eric wanted sex and Kristen wanted words. This is a clear example of different needs. It's been said that a woman's greatest erogenous zone is her heart and often her greatest need is for loving words. The fact is, sexual intimacy is reached when other layers of intimacy are in place. We talked about the dimensions of intimacy earlier, including social intimacy, recreational intimacy, and intellectual intimacy. As Kenneth Chafin writes, "The modern notion that sex is what gives meaning to the rest of the relationship has it backward. It is the sharing of the experience of life together as husband and wife that makes sex more meaningful."[25]

We also are learning that many layers of our lives affect our desire for or enjoyment of our sexual relationship. They are:

- **Physical differences:** Most couples are unaware of how powerfully physical differences can affect the quality of their sex life. For instance, sex researchers note that when it comes to sexual readiness and arousal, a husband can become fully aroused in ninety seconds, whereas a wife can take between fifteen and thirty minutes.
- **Family background:** Both men and women are greatly influenced by their families' attitudes toward sex. Some grew up in families where sexual facts were discussed openly, while others grew up in families where sex was considered shameful. These differences can prevent a loving response.
- **Culture:** Movies, television, and books can confuse and hinder a couple's sexual life with unrealistic expectations and descriptions that are anything but normal. To the degree that a couple exposes themselves to this cultural confusion, this layer of intimacy can cause problems.
- **Prior sexual experiences:** An increasing number of couples have had some sexual encounters before marriage. Their feelings of guilt, regret, and remorse can cause "emo-

tional scar tissue" that can block a person from fully enjoying marital sex.

- **Present experiences:** A "hard day at the office" or a "rough time with the kids" can significantly reduce a person's capacity to feel caring or loving toward a spouse.
- **Physical and emotional needs:** Certain needs, such as an illness, can soak up sexual desire.
- **Spiritual needs:** Spiritual intimacy between a couple connects them at the deepest level and adds to the enjoyment of and involvement in sex.[26]

In general, couples' sex lives improve when they recognize the many layers that contribute to their sexual intimacy. They also improve their satisfaction as they learn what works in their busy schedules, and as they openly communicate their expectations about sex to their mates. Admittedly, this isn't always easy. Many good books and resources are available on this topic, and they are listed in the Mobilizer and Recommended Reading sections of this chapter.

Act Out Your Love

It's often the little things that add up and set the tone for intimacy in marriage. Little things put into action, that is. Here's a whole list of little things that can add up to a big difference in bringing intimacy to your relationship:

Awareness. How often do you look—really *look*—at the one you married, and see—really *see*—that person? He walks into the room. Do you even raise your head to greet each other?

Both of us have a number of things on our plates other than the kids, and we have put them aside to concentrate on each other.

She crawls into bed. Do you tear your eyes away from the sports program on television?

We have two choices in relationships: we can notice or we can numb out. Which do you choose in your marriage? Not sure? Well, compare your level of awareness to how you notice your children. How do you respond when your son or daughter climbs in the car after preschool? Do you notice his body language? Do you beam and brighten with adoration at the things she says? Some of us are better at noticing our children than our spouses.

Anne Ortlund challenges, "Get in the habit of checking each other's *face* every time you encounter each other, even every few minutes."[27] Notice a new haircut, or eyes or body language that say "I had a hard day." Then let your spouse know you notice. Comment. Question. Touch. Acknowledge. Respond. Insert yourself into the life of your mate the way you do into the life of your child. You will be able to watch your intimacy grow.

Spontaneity. One secret of a happy marriage is spontaneity. "Love, like a newspaper, must be made up new every morning. Yesterday's love and yesterday's paper may have been absorbing, but today they are as flat and lifeless as leftover soda water."[28]

Being spontaneous means acting naturally, without self-consciousness. Synonyms to *spontaneous* are words like *enthusiasm, nerve, ardor, zest, impulsiveness,* and *initiative.* Keep him guessing. Surprise her with a spontaneous kiss. Add the ingredient of spontaneity to your love routine.

Giving. "No marriage relationship can remain close if the man and wife do not express gratitude to one another," according to Jim and Jeri White.[29] Giving is a quality that enriches both the giver and receiver. When husband and wife give of themselves and give gratitude to each other, they deepen their intimacy.

When asked about some of the ways couples with children can keep romance alive in their marriages, respondents to our questionnaire show the importance of awareness, spontaneity, and giving. Here's a sampling of their answers:

From husbands . . .

- Send love notes
- Plan surprise dates
- Schedule time away alone

- Bring home flowers
- Be goofy; do childlike things—play, dance, ride a tandem bike
- Give foot massages
- Turn off the TV after the kids go to bed and talk—or whatever
- Say "I love you"

From wives . . .

- Always say "hello" and "good-bye" with a kiss
- Touch each other with neck massages and back rubs
- Hold hands
- Wink at each other
- Put the kids to bed early
- Talk about grown-up things, not just about the kids
- Nap together in the afternoon

CONCLUSION

Every marriage needs intimacy, but, as with commitment and interdependence, children test and change the meaning of intimacy. The marriage mobile bounces out of control as a couple loses the only-you-and-me kind of intimacy that existed before children. But here's the good news: In reestablishing a sense of intimacy, the marriage grows stronger, and the investment of effort pays off with a deeper relationship that will endure and thrive in the other seasons of life.

MOBILIZER #1: LIGHTEN UP

To keep your marriage brimming with love in the loving cup,
when you're wrong, admit it; when you're right, shut up.

OGDEN NASH

MOBILIZER #2: PRESCRIPTION FOR A HEALTHY LOVE LIFE

1. **Take care of yourself.** If you are going to make
your marriage a priority and be the parent you want to
be, you first need to learn to pace yourself. So without
guilt, consider ways you could be good to yourself. For
instance, take fifteen minutes each day to sit, read, reflect, or do whatever you want to do; get eight hours
of sleep; hire a babysitter and do whatever you want to
do for a couple of hours.
2. **Be good to your marriage.** Remember, parenting
is a temporary job. Each kid will be out of the house in
about eighteen years. But your mate is there for life!
What can you do now to make your marriage a high
priority? For instance, tell your honey five reasons why
you love him or her; eat a bowl of ice cream together
after the kids are in bed; put sticky notes everywhere
with personal messages.

3. **Let your marriage be good to your children.**
When children grow up in happy, intact, functional
families with parents who love each other, they uncon-
sciously learn the roles they will later need in marriage
and parenthood. As you focus on your marriage, you
mentor your children in these ways.

- **Your marriage provides stability.** A strong marriage
significantly enhances children's security and stability by
letting them know that the unconditional, lifelong love
modeled between parents also applies to them. Even parents arguing and then making up demonstrates that life
goes on and love is not diminished in the face of disagreements and stress.
- **Your marriage sets the tone.** The way you relate to
each other sets the atmosphere in your home. If you ha-
bitually joke and laugh together, your home will be a fun
place to be, and your children will learn how to laugh
and enjoy life. Conversely, if your kids only see you
argue, they are more likely to argue. What is the general
tone of your home? Think about how you relate to each
other. If your marriage sets a positive tone, your children
will be benefactors!
- **Your marriage helps shape relationships.** What did
your parents model to you? Were they loving and affectionate with each other? Usually you will have picked up
many ways of relating that were taught to you (either
consciously or not) by your parents. If you work to build
a strong, loving marriage, your children will, by watching you, learn how to give and receive love, how to nurture, how to resolve conflict, how to communicate, and
how to live. What a legacy to give your children.[30]

MOBILIZER #3: DATE YOUR MATE

Many couples rekindle their sense of intimacy by dating each other again, as they did in the beginning of their relationship. For instance, they set aside Friday nights for alone time together. The plans might be as simple as having an in-house date, including a late-night dinner together in front of the fireplace after the kids are in bed. Or the plans might be as elaborate as having a weekly arrangement with a reliable babysitter, so the date always means getting away from home. Here's how some couples make the idea work.

Start a Dating Club

You can build a closer friendship while helping other couples do the same, by organizing your own dating club! Follow these simple six steps:

1. Find several other couples who want to develop more togetherness in their marriage. Think of like-minded friends (other couples at church, at work, in your parenting or couples' group).

2. Choose a date night for the group. Once a week, every other week—even once a month could be really enriching!

3. Find regular child care. This may be the most daunting task, but it's not impossible. Consider challenging your church to offer free or low-cost child care once a month so couples in the church can fortify their marriages. If you belong to a parenting support group that provides child care during meetings, perhaps the child-care workers would be willing to make themselves available for your group's date night. Get your own individual sitter or consolidate kids at

someone's home and bring in several trusted sitters. Keep brainstorming until you find something that works for you.

4. Pick a theme for each date. This will help you stay on target and will help you develop new common interests as a couple and as a couples' group. Choose a book or resource that offers themes for dates. (For instance, *10 Great Dates to Revitalize Your Marriage* [Zondervan, 1997] contains tear-out pages for ten dates with marriage-enriching themes. Short video "date launches" are also available.)

5. Take turns with the other couples in facilitating your fifteen- to twenty-minute "date launch." Introduce the theme for the date and encourage couples to have fun!

6. Then have fun dating your mate! And don't forget to come back and pick up your kids![31]

MOBLILIZER #4: PLAN YOUR OWN MARRIAGE RETREAT

For many husbands and wives, the only way to truly rekindle their sense of intimacy is to get away from home for an overnight or a weekend at least once or twice a year. Sound impossible? Not if you recognize the importance of this alone time together and plan ahead. Trade weekends with another couple or send the kids to grandparents.

Guidelines

A few guidelines will help you maximize your time together with meaningful conversations that lead to the kind of emotional and romantic bonding that might be missing in your hectic routines at home:

- Agree ahead of time whether you will or will not discuss any major conflict issues.
- Commit to really listen to each other. Don't interrupt.
- Plan an agenda of nonconflict conversation topics. For instance, talk about how you've both changed since becoming parents, and your dreams for the future. Try to talk about each other, not only about your child or children.

Conversation Starters

Here are some ideas to get you talking together about who you are and who you hope to become as husband and wife, and mom and dad. Answer them for yourself, and then switch and try to answer them for your spouse. Afterwards, compare notes.

Self-disclosure: I am _____ (Fill in ten descriptions each. Most start with . . . a man, woman, husband, wife, but move on to more personal descriptions, such as . . . sensitive, assertive, etc.)

My husband (or wife) sees me as _____.

Priorities: If our house suddenly caught on fire, I would first grab   .

If I had six weeks left to live, I would spend my time ____
_____.

Dreams and Goals: If I were to receive an award in five years for being outstanding, the award would be for   _____
_____.

My idea of the best kind of vacation is   _____
_____.

Relationship: I feel most loved by you when you _____
_____.

I could be a better husband (or wife) by   _____
_____.

I love you because _____

_____.

(Hopefully, this will be the longest answer.)

MOBILIZER # 5: PRACTICE CONFLICT RESOLUTION

Conflicts in marriage are inevitable, so plan ahead about how you and your spouse will resolve your inevitable conflicts. Then, when you hit a bump in the road, you have a map to help you negotiate through the rough spot. Without a plan, you might withdraw, leaving conflicts unsettled. Or the conflict might escalate into a free-for-all of put-downs and angry comments which you can't take back. Here are some guidelines to will help you.

Work It Out

- **Recognize marriage as a "we" business.** Your relationship will shrivel if it becomes a matter of only two "I's." Focus on what's best for "us," not just for "me."
- **Process the data as quickly as you can.** Conflict prolonged grows more dangerous. Get it out in the open. Deal with all the important facts and feelings then and there.
- **Stick to the subject.** Don't turn a disagreement into a competition by resurrecting unrelated or old grievances. Resolve one problem at a time.
- **Don't intimidate.** Never threaten by using a loud voice, a dominating physical posture, a list of consequences, or a barrage of emotional bombshells in the heat of the moment. It's destructive.

- **Banish name-calling.** If a description is meant to depreciate or demean, you'll just end up hurting your partner and trying to apologize later.
- **Turn up your listening sensitivity.** Instead of speaking and defending your position, pay attention, restate your spouse's view, and evaluate its merits.
- **Practice give-and-take.** You won't be taken advantage of if you both regularly and graciously compromise.
- **Celebrate every victory.** Every time you resolve a conflict, no matter how small, give yourselves credit for improving your marital skills.[32]

Fight Fair

Rules for the match:
1. Keep it honest.
2. Keep it under control.
3. Keep it timed right.
4. Keep it positive.
5. Keep it tactful.
6. Keep it private.
7. Keep it cleaned up.

Most important: When you're wrong, admit it.[33]

MOBILIZER #6: HOW TO HAVE GOOD SEX

Intimacy includes many levels of closeness in a relationship and leads to a good sexual relationship. Here are some tips to help you increase your sexual satisfaction in marriage.

Recognize the Common Killers of Good Sex

- Fatigue
- Unrealistic expectations
- Comparisons
- Criticism
- Inflexibility
- Using sex as a reward or consequence
- Dishonesty and "faking it"

Ten Crucial Factors for a Great Sex Life

Dr. Clifford and Joyce Penner are experts on the topic of sexual adjustment in marriage. When asked, "What percentage of couples can attain a mutually satisfying sexual relationship?" they answered, "100 percent of them."

When asked, "How many attain this kind of mutual satisfaction quite naturally, without having to work at it?" they answered, "About one third." Here are their suggestions about how to work at achieving a mutually satisfying sexual relationship.

1. **The most vital factor in producing a great sexual relationship in marriage revolves around the role of the man.** Sexual patterns in a marriage begin to change dramatically when the man changes, even when the woman may be the one hindering a vital sexual relationship. So even though "it takes two to tango," as they say, the greater responsibility for improvement rests with the husband.

2. **The man must move in the direction of the woman's needs.** He needs to become acutely aware of as many of her spiritual and emotional needs as he possibly can. His awareness, obviously, will increase in direct proportion to his ability to listen to her.

3. **The woman needs to learn how to take.** She needs to listen carefully to her body and then seek what will satisfy her desires. Though wives are typically eager to please their husbands, they should be ready to receive an equal degree of pleasure.

4. **The woman must feel free to lead in the sexual experience.** There's an Old Testament passage from the Song of Songs that teaches a three-step process that leads to dramatic sexual improvement. First, the man affirms the woman; he talks freely about her virtues. Second, the woman takes the lead; she proceeds at her speed, and she lets the man know her thoughts and desires at all times. Third, the man responds; he listens carefully to what she says, and he acts only in response to her desires.

5. **The man must progress very s-l-o-w-l-y.** In other words, the man must slow way down.

6. **The man needs to remain flexible, without a set "agenda" for how things are supposed to go.** His "guidance system" should be his wife. Many men try to get the recipe down and then follow it. This almost never works because a woman's sexual desires, needs, and responses cannot be predicted from one time to the next.

7. **Both the husband and wife need to be into the sexual process for the pleasure of it (not for the result of it).** The goal of sex is to build intimacy with your spouse. The secret is to enjoy both your own body and your partner's. If climax is not reached for either partner, it shouldn't be seen as a big disappointment or failure.

8. **If one of the partners was the victim of sexual abuse during childhood, there must be healing from the trauma.** The victims of abuse often carry into marriage emotional scars that hinder free and uninhib-

ited sexual expression. . . . Most often this healing process requires a professional to help face the abuse, grieve the losses involved, and regain a sense of wholeness.

9. **Mutual satisfaction is the expectation in every sexual experience.** The woman must be able to allow an orgasm if she wants one. The fundamental requirement for satisfaction, however, is a deep sense of interpersonal closeness and warmth.

10. **It is vital that both partners know how the body works sexually.** Don't laugh! Most people enter marriage with many misconceptions about how things work. A thorough understanding will make expectations far more reasonable, and couples won't suffer from the disappointment and disillusionment that come from unrealistic desires and demands.[34]

A Wife's Guide to Saying Yes or No to Making Love

If you give yourself permission to say no, you have also given yourself permission to say yes even when you're not quite in the mood. You have given yourself permission to make an unselfish choice and to consider your husband's needs, on any given night, as more important than your own. You have allowed yourself the privilege of making a small sacrifice for someone you love. The best marriages, in fact, are filled with moments such as these, shining moments of self-sacrifice on the part of both partners!

So . . .

- Say YES when you want to make love.
- Say YES when you don't necessarily want to make love, but you know it will bring you joy to meet the needs of your husband.
- Say LATER when making love at that very moment will leave you feeling trapped or resentful.[35]

MOBILIZER #7: TEACH YOUR CHILDREN TO RESPECT YOUR MARRIAGE RELATIONSHIP

1. **Create your own private space.** It's critical that you have your own private space in your home. And we do mean physical space—whether it's your bedroom, study, or even the master bathroom. It's a space where children must have special permission to enter. Your private space can be a sanctuary where you can be alone and focus on loving each other. It serves as your refuge from the overwhelming needs and chaos of family life.

2. **Cultivate your own private times.** We suggest two types of private times: *adult time*, when your kids may still be around but you aren't focusing on them, and *alone time*, when your children are safely in bed or otherwise occupied in their own rooms, and you can concentrate on loving.

3. **Be openly affectionate.** Children need to realize that the relationship between their mother and father is distinct and not dependent on them. The level of affection you're comfortable displaying will vary from couple to couple, but remember, it's healthy for your children to overhear loving remarks and to see you hold hands, cuddle on the couch, or kiss.

4. **Build friendships with other adults.** Through your interaction with other grown-ups, you'll be providing your children with models of marriage relationships and adult friendships that broaden their frame of reference. Your kids will also see that you two aren't the only adults in the world who like to hold hands or cuddle, thereby making you more like everyone else and less creepy.[36]

MOBILIZER #8: GIFTS YOU CAN GIVE YOUR MARRIAGE

One of the challenges of life in this season of raising young children is to find creative and meaningful ways to deepen your love life in the midst of hectic days. Pause and think about the gifts you can give your marriage. In most cases, they are gifts that cost nothing but are worth everything.

- **Gift of Companionship:** My willingness to do things together, even if that means learning a new activity or sacrificing some of my own time.
- **Gift of Humility:** My desire to be able to admit that I'm not always right, and that I need to change in some areas of my life.
- **Gift of Time:** Time for me to be alone; time for my friends; time to sleep.
- **Gift of Acceptance:** An acceptance of who I am and who I am becoming as I grow and change.
- **Gift of Encouragement:** My commitment to help my spouse become all God created him or her to be.
- **Gift of Forgiveness:** My willingness to forgive my spouse, to get over it and then get on with it.
- **Gift of Flexibility:** My desire to be open to new schedules and new ways of doing things.
- **Gift of Laughter:** My pledge to lighten up and have fun and play together.
- **Gift of a Shared Future:** My hope to dream and continue to plan our future together.

MOBILIZER #9: AN EXAMPLE OF PERFECT INTIMACY

Perhaps *perfect* intimacy is unrealistic for one human to offer another. Only Jesus offers us this kind of love, unconditionally. When we have such love from Jesus, we can love each other more perfectly. Here's an example of that offer.

> You can be whoever you are, express all your thoughts and feelings with absolute confidence. You do not have to be fearful that love will be taken away. You will not be punished for your openness or honesty. There is no admission price to my love, no rental fees or installment payments to be made. There may be days when disagreements and disturbing emotions may come between us. There may be times when psychological or physical miles may lie between us. But I have given you the word of my commitment. I have set my life on a course. I will not go back on my word to you. So feel free to be yourself, to tell me of your negative and positive reactions, of your warm and cold feelings. I cannot always predict my reactions or guarantee my strength, but one thing I do know and I do want you to know: I will not reject you! I am committed to your growth and happiness. I will always love you.[37]

Questions to Ask Each Other

- What does intimacy mean to us?
- How has our level of intimacy changed since we had children?
- What's the difference between intimacy and romance?
- What are some of the greatest causes of stress in our relationship?
- How can we minimize those issues?

- How well do we understand each other? What's an example of where each of us felt understood and misunderstood in the last week?
- In what ways do we fight unfairly? How can we help each other to fight more fairly?
- How comfortable are we talking about sex, and why? How can we make each other more comfortable?
- What one idea could we incorporate from Mobilizer #6 to improve our sex life?
- What are some specific ways we can keep romance alive in our marriage?

Recommended Reading

10 Great Dates to Revitalize Your Marriage, David and Claudia Arp

The Act of Marriage, Tim and Beverly LaHaye

Communication: Key to Your Marriage, H. Norman Wright

The Gift of Sex, Dr. Clifford and Joyce Penner

Great Sexpectations, Robert Barnes

Intended for Pleasure, Dr. Ed and Gayle Wheat

Intimate Issues: 21 Questions Christian Women Ask About Sex, Linda Dillow and Lorraine Pintus

The Language of Love, Gary Smalley and John Trent

Love Life for Parents, David and Claudia Arp

Pillow Talk: The Intimate Marriage from A to Z, Karen Scalf Linamen

To Understand Each Other, Paul Tournier

Five

Mission
RETHINK YOUR PURPOSE

What makes this family a family?

J on leaned back in the driver's seat and accelerated the car as he pulled into the line of traffic on the freeway. "That was a good weekend, wasn't it?" he turned to question his wife, Rachel, who sat next to him in the car.

"Yeah, honey, it was great. The whole Thanksgiving feast was perfect—turkey *and* all the rest of the food. I don't know how your mother makes it look so easy. And your sister is amazing with those three children. She seems so patient all the time!"

Behind them in her car seat, two-year-old Meagan dozed. While she refused a nap at home, she always dozed in the car. Thank goodness.

Something had been niggling at Rachel for the last few days. Maybe it was her pregnancy and the fact that they would become a family of four in a few months, but she'd been thinking lots lately about the unique qualities that made certain families appear stronger than others. Jon's parents seemed to have such a *solid* marriage and family life. They shared an obvious commitment to each other, and their time together meant so much to all of them. Both Jon's brother, still a bachelor, and his well-settled sister and her husband "plugged in" to the security of home when they returned, even as adults. Rachel longed to repeat this pattern in their family, but how would they go about it? In a few short weeks, she and Jon would be spending their first major holiday alone, by their choice. Her family was practically nonexistent and his was going to his sister's which was more than five hundred miles away. Rachel felt apprehensive. How would she pull off all the Christmas responsibilities, especially while holding down her job?

Jon wasn't crazy about her working, but they both knew they couldn't get by on his income alone. Several questions ran through her mind: *How much would they spend on Meagan's gifts and what toys would they choose for her? What traditions would they start? What would Jon expect of their family Christmas since he came from such a seemingly perfect family?*

Rachel turned towards her husband and started to voice some of these concerns. Jon listened and then offered his usual nonchalant comment. "Don't worry about it, Rachel. It'll all work out." But even as he said those words, he was surprised to feel his own questions surfacing. He and Rachel had disagreed about where Meagan should sleep at his parents' house. Rachel thought the child should sleep with them since she was in unfamiliar surroundings. But Jon felt they should be stricter and encourage Meagan to adapt to a new spot. His mom had her own opinion and didn't hesitate to share it, which miffed Rachel. Now that he thought about it, these issues about parenting and in-law relationships were even more important than holiday traditions and presents for Meagan.

"Maybe we should talk about some of these things, Rachel. We have a couple of hours of drive time today with Meagan asleep." But two hours later, as they pulled up to their home, Jon and Rachel realized they had made little progress in sorting through the tangle of these family issues. Some of them made them both defensive. They'd disagreed about money and Rachel's job. They'd found common ground on some issues of parenting and priorities. They hadn't even talked about Christmas presents and holiday activities. As they unloaded the car, toting baby paraphernalia and sacks of Thanksgiving leftovers into the kitchen, the big question still remained unanswered: "What makes this family a family, anyway?"

WHAT MAKES YOUR FAMILY A "FAMILY"?

The definition of family has been tossed around and tweaked for generations, often to fit the cultural norms of the time. Sometimes family is defined by relationships, sometimes by function and purpose. Often it is best described by a family photo album rather than a bunch of words.

Most commonly, family is recognized as society's most basic and durable unit. Ideally, it is a safe and secure place where people can grow and transmit values. It is designed to accomplish good in the lives of those involved. In the book *Is There a Family in the House?* Kenneth Chafin describes a family simply as "a balanced environment designed by God for the growth of human beings."[1] That "balance" is further defined by the way life is lived in the family, with a proper blending of roles, freedom and responsibility, love, commitment, and hard work. Here's another definition from Neil Clark Warren in his book *Forever My Love*:

> When there is love between a husband and wife, and where there is strong respect for the children born out of that love, the result is sure to be a family that can relate to one another in deeply meaningful ways. When this kind of connectedness happens within a secure atmosphere, the many shades of love that result almost always make for an overwhelmingly beautiful human fabric. We call this fabric a family.[2]

Since we've had children we've added a significant shared goal (raising kids) which has brought a clearer sense of unity and purpose.

— ✻ —

We're a family unit now, with branches to our roots.

— ✻ —

Marriage is a partnership; as parents we've become a team with common goals.

Children Bring Gifts to the Family

A family is a structure of relationships, bonded together by common purposes. In the marriage mobile, a couple represents a family, with the addition of children bringing a whole new set of relationships. Within the context of these new relationships, children change and challenge the identification of common purposes, as we saw with Jon, and Rachel, and Meagan approaching their first Christmas alone as a family. Children also deepen the commitment and interdependence of the relationships in the family.

Children bring focus to the family. The addition of children in a family almost always forces a husband and wife to think about what matters most to them and what they want to pass on to their children. As a couple, they might have lived together with a hang-loose attitude of freedom and spontaneity, but once they have children they begin thinking about the deeper issues of life—what they want to stand for and leave to the world that is beyond themselves.

The most difficult change we've faced is learning our new roles as parents.

— ✻ —

Since becoming a parent I've realized that our children reflect not only our strengths but also our weaknesses.

Children hold us accountable to what we value. Children cause us to look more carefully at ourselves, our marriages, and our lives. They motivate us to identify what we value, and then they force us to "walk our talk" as they watch us and mimic us and evaluate what we say and do.

A Family Needs a Mission

Families can grow in a take-it-as-it-comes-and-let-it-happen style, or they can grow through intentional effort. Most of us don't realize what shape and direction our families are taking until we stand back and look at the bigger picture and objectively consider what we're creating. Most families need motivation to take the time to figure out what is important to them and how to implement such values. For Jon and Rachel, the motivation came from the impending birth of a second child and the thought of spending their first Christmas alone together.

If a family is not shaped by a defined purpose, it may grow haphazardly and keep the marriage mobile swinging out of balance. Therefore, every family needs a mission. There's an old saying, "If you aim for nothing, you're bound to hit it." A family mission helps us aim for *something* with intentionality. It may or may not be written down, but the important part is that the mission is recognized and understood by the family members.

Two main ingredients make up a family mission. First, the family mission defines *a reason to exist.* The mission answers the question, What makes us a family, distinctly different from a random gathering of people? Secondly, the family mission defines *a legacy to leave.* What do we want to leave our children and our world because we were a family? Answers come as you clarify what's important to you as a family.

FAMILY VALUES

In order to define what makes your family a family, reexamine your marriage relationship for the values and goals that bring you stability. In other words, define the meaning of your family by defining your combined values as a couple. What is important to you as a couple? What are your shared passions?

Now that we are parents, it's hard—growing up so fast and spelling out responsibilities and expectations.

— ✳ —

Agreeing on parenting and the best methods to reach life goals has been difficult for us.

— ✳ —

We had to decide on priorities for our home and how we would work together to avoid the same problems we experienced as children.

What are you aiming for together, beyond yourselves? "Life has taught us that love does not consist of gazing at each other but in looking outward together in the same direction," writes Antoine de Saint Exupery.[3]

Management guru Stephen Covey suggests that families, as well as individuals, set goals by beginning with the end in mind. This means "to start with a clear understanding of your destination. It means to know where you're going so that you better understand where you are now and so that the steps you take are always in the right direction."[4]

Think about it this way: What do you want your family to look like in five years? In ten years? Peer even further ahead. In twenty years, when your children are grown and hopefully handling life on their own, what do you hope they are offering the world as the legacy of your family? What kind of an adult do you hope your child will become? Begin with the end in mind by focusing on the end result. Those descriptions help us define our values and clarify just what will make our family a family.

Henri Nouwen encourages us about the value of goal-setting. "Without a clear goal," he says, "our lives become fragmented into many tasks and obligations that drain us and leave us with a feeling of exhaustion and uselessness."[5]

Your family mission will be formed as you define your family values in several major areas. Let's take them one at a time.

Marriage

Marriage means having common goals and having someone to work, play, rest, and recreate with.

— ✶ —

My idea of "clean" is my wife's idea of "messy."

When considering the marriage part of the family mission, consider the priority given to the marriage relationship in a family with children, and ask yourself how that priority might be lived out in time and effort. "Show me a man and a woman who have children, and I will show you a man and woman who need more than ever to nurture their relationship," writes Neil Clark Warren in *Forever My Love*.[6] Warren goes on to explain that "romance requires personal time. There is never a time when two people can keep their love growing and prospering without plenty of energy spent relating to each other individually and intimately."[7]

He summarizes, "A great marriage provides optimal conditions for a child to do well. And a child's success often contributes to the health of a marriage. . . . The best way to build great families is to build great marriages."[8] In defining your marriage goals and values, consider the necessary ingredients of married love, such as respect, encouragement, kindness, patience, and humility. Often these are the same values you want to pass on to your children, and as such they become part of the parenting mission.

Parenting

Parenting is one of the most important tasks we face, yet the plethora of parenting approaches and techniques is enough to spin any marriage mobile out of control. Take a father who was raised in a

We're trying to talk openly about our expectations, especially with tasks with the baby.

— ✗ —

We need consistency in dealing with the children.

permissive environment where he learned by natural consequences; add a mother who was reared in a militaristic home where "Yes, Ma'am" and "Yes, Sir" were required in response to every parental command, and the result is complete confusion of values. While not all couples share such divergent parenting backgrounds, each spouse does bring his or her own experience and perspective to parenting. Melding a united mission can be difficult for any couple—but well worth the effort. "I encourage parents to recognize what a vital part child rearing can play in their lives together," writes Neil Clark Warren in his book *The Triumphant Marriage*. "When they take it on as partners, when they see what a sacred privilege it is, when they come to recognize that rearing great kids is a goal worth pursuing, they are headed toward something wonderful."[9]

As you work to establish your family mission as partners in parenting, consider one foundational question: What is the goal of your parenting? Once you clarify this, the daily applications can be put in place.

For example, in their book *Raising Great Kids*, Henry Cloud and John Townsend identify the goal of parenting as creating children with character who will become successful adults. In implementing that goal, parents want to:

> create love with a spouse, which can transfer down to
>   another generation;
> pass on their values to others;
> create a warm and caring family context;
> have fun with their kids;
> contribute something to the world.[10]

You might express your parenting goals a bit differently, but if you're having trouble identifying these goals, try standing back from the daily tasks of parenting, and consider this question: When your child grows up, what do you hope to have done in that child's life? What qualities do you hope your child will have? Your answer will help you clarify your goals.

Traditions

We've decided to put "fun" in an actual time slot in our daily planner.

Traditions tie a family together. They represent a sense of history and security because they grow out of "the way we always do things." James Dobson writes, "The great value of traditions is that they give a family a sense of identity, of belongingness. . . . That we're not just a cluster of people living together in a house, but we're a family that's conscious of it uniqueness, of its personality, of its character, and its heritage. And the special relationship within the family of love and companionship makes us a unit that has an identity, that has, as I say, a personality."[11]

A family sets traditions based on their values. Many are passed down from generation to generation and combined to fit this new family. Mom and Dad combine the way they celebrated Christmas as children, deciding whether to open presents on Christmas Eve (like she did as a child) or on Christmas morning (like he did as a child). The compromise also widens to embrace this generation's family values, such as the decision to open presents on Christmas morning, after a birthday party for Jesus.

Choose traditions, rituals, and celebrations that you want to reflect your family's values and personality. How about waffles every Sunday morning? Bonanza birthday celebrations that truly honor the uniqueness of the birthday person? Summer family reunions? Notes of encouragement and Bible verses on the refrigerator door? Grace before meals? A humorous family photo on the annual Christmas card? Pick the ones that shape your family and make it unique, and hold on to them as long as they continue to do so.

Work

In today's world, there is no one right way to define a family when it comes to work. We're surrounded by many models. Two-career couples. Stay-at-home moms. Mr. Moms. Part-time everything.

My husband is so wrapped up in his work he doesn't hear me.

— *x** —

We need to agree on whether I should work or not. It's hard for me to give up my work.

While the options are staggering, there are a few principles to consider when making a decision for your family mission regarding work.

Children need their parents. Research has shown that a child's environment from birth to age three helps determine brain structure and the ability to learn.

A 1994 Carnegie Corporation report finds that brain development before age one is

- more rapid and extensive,
- more vulnerable to environmental influence, and
- longer lasting than previously realized.

Further,

- The environment affects the number of brain cells, connections among them, and the way connections are wired.
- Early stress has a negative impact on brain development.[12]

Choices regarding work should be carefully interplayed with the developmental needs of each child and reexamined regularly with this priority in mind. Both father and mother have a responsibility to put their child's developmental needs before their jobs and outside activities as best they can during these foundational years.

Take a seasonal approach. When making decisions regarding work, remember that the stage of raising young children is just that: a stage. We can "sequence" our work lives, narrowing the scope of our pursuits so as to give priority to children when they are young.

Include "homework" in your mission analysis. When making decisions regarding work, it's easy to look only outside the home. Yet work done within the home can be just as distracting as the work done away. How often stay-at-home moms believe their focus is their children when in actuality they've allowed housework and volunteer work to overtake their hours! And how common it is for a couple to share the role of breadwinner and yet segregate household chores only to the woman so that she, in fact, holds down the equivalent of two jobs.

I have to decide to accomplish one or two fewer things each day than I really want to.

Take care to review the hours spent in home businesses, housekeeping, business commuting, and extracurricular activities to assess where your focus is and where it should be during these child-rearing years.

Money

Decisions regarding work lead every couple to one of the greatest challenges in every marriage: the making and management of money. In fact, the moms and dads we surveyed report that disagreements about money comprises the second greatest problem area of disagreement in their marriages. (Communication ranked as the greatest problem.) During these years of ne-

We've gone from a two-income family to a one-income family, and are constantly examining priorities, spending, etc.

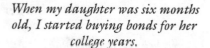

When my daughter was six months old, I started buying bonds for her college years.

gotiation of work-related decisions, money issues can take on disproportionate power.

Here are some suggestions for making you the master of your money—instead of the other way around.

- **Talk about money.** Many couples are so uncomfortable with the subject of finances that they deny them altogether. Together, set goals for buying a house or other major purchases. Clarify what is "essential" and "nonessential" regarding your purchases. Talk openly and honestly about what is important to you financially and listen to the views of your spouse. Then cooperate,

which often means yielding "what's best for me" in favor
of "what's best for the marriage."

- **Have both partners aware of the family finances.** Too
  often in the past, husbands have made the major financial decisions, leaving the wives ignorant or just unin-
  volved. Such a pattern inbreeds financial incompetence.
  Instead, share the knowledge of and the responsibility for
  financial matters.

- **Take turns paying bills.** There's no better way to share in
  the responsibility for finances than to share in the alloca-
  tion of them. Switch off the bill-paying from month to
  month and watch communication grow!

- **Refuse debt.** Recognize early on that debt is not a solution for a pinched budget. Agree together how credit
  cards will be used and paid off each month and then hold
  each other accountable to your guidelines.

The Larger Family

*I need to know that my husband at
least cares about my side of the family.*

— ✸ —

*I want my wife to stand up to her
mother more often.*

All families face sensi-
tive issues involving relationships with in-laws,
grandparents, aunts and
uncles and cousins. Some
face issues with blended
families. How do we en-
courage right relationships? How do we honor our parents,
while also having appropriate boundaries? How do we accept
advice and criticism? How do we teach our children respect for
family members we don't respect? How can we clarify who is
"Mom" when there are two to keep straight in this blended
family? What can we do to strengthen ties with grandparents
without letting them "run the show"? What do we value in our
relationships with our extended families? Such issues and questions about the extended family are sometimes sticky and deli-
cate, and yet vital to the expression of who we are as a family.

Beyond the Family

Part of our calling as a family is to reach out beyond our own worlds to serve others. What is your family's contribution to the world at large? What is our responsibility to others who are not in our family, to our neighborhood, our country, and our environment? The fact is, though we raise our children in our homes, we don't cocoon them there; we want them to venture out and learn to live well and responsibly in the world beyond our homes. Children develop their fear or familiarity with the world around them from the way they are brought up in their families. Does your family interact with your neighbors? Does your family interact with people who are different from you, people of different ages or cultural backgrounds? Do you help your children participate in the flood or hurricane relief drives? Does your family visit retirement homes? Does your family practice recycling to save the environment?

Your family's orientation toward the world at large may also be based in your family's faith decisions. Is God important to your family? How so? What do you need to do to explore your faith more fully? How can you lead your children to a clearer understanding of who God is and his purposes for the world?

Widening your circle as a family will help give you and your children a clear direction for the future.

MAKING A FAMILY MISSION STATEMENT

Once the subject matter is clarified, it's time to move on to actually create your own family's mission statement. Many couples create a family mission statement early on in their marriages. Some premarital counselors encourage this task as part of a couple's preparation for marriage; other families find that, years later, it has simply emerged from family mottoes or familiar family sayings. The bottom-line question is:

> *I need a partner to help raise our children to love and follow the Lord.*

"What will be the purpose of your family?" The identification of that purpose, and the plan for achieving it is what makes up the mission statement.

A mission statement is an expression of belief. As Covey puts it, "your mission statement becomes your constitution, the solid expression of your vision and values. It becomes the criterion by which you measure everything else in your life."[13]

Such a family definition is not formed overnight. Rather, it comes through careful and often prayerful thought and processing of who you are and what really matters to you as a family unit. Over time, as your family grows and changes, that definition will need to be adjusted as well.

Once we had kids, we discovered that all our planning on how we were going to raise them suddenly changed.

Consider the following information when defining and creating your family's mission statement.

Mentor Models

When you're in the business of defining your family purpose, it's enlightening to take a look at how others are defining theirs, to sidle up alongside other couples who are just a few steps further along in their marriages and families than you are! Observe how these couples handle their children. Watch how coworkers juggle home and work. Watch extended family members to see how they balance their responsibilities and how they invest their money. Get close to an older couple at church or in your neighborhood and notice how they relate to each other and continue to invest in their marriage.

Learn from the models of marriage around you and shape your own family by their good and bad examples. What elements bring harmony and balance in their marriage mobiles? Where do you see them out of kilter—and why?

Leave a Legacy

Another helpful tool to jump-start your thinking and clarify a family mission is to consider the legacy you want your family to leave. We create a legacy by weaving the inheritance of values we've received from our family of origin with that of our present family.

Begin by looking through what you've been given by your own parents. You may have much you want to discard, but identify the values and principles you would like to integrate into your family life today. What were your parents' priorities? Did they teach you honesty? Did they put relationships above possessions or career success? Did they celebrate family milestones well? Did they express loyalty to other family members?

H. Norman Wright suggests, "Perhaps instead of waiting for the family history to be shared in a eulogy, we could discover it now and preserve it for both ourselves and other family members."[14] Think of some of the family stories that exemplify the values you've inherited from your parents and grandparents.

Then, after looking back at your own family history, look forward. Consider what you want to contribute to the world and future generations from your own family. There is an old saying that "the greatest use of life is to spend it for something that will outlast it."[15]

Edith Schaeffer asserts that a family is a "museum of memories." And she considers herself to have a fantastic job because she is a curator in that museum of memories.[16] Today we are creating the indelible memories that will live in the hearts and souls of our children and their children for all of their tomorrows. Do you want your children to carry pictures of love and respect and loyalty and bonded relationships? If so, identify those as values now, live them out in your life experience, and you will pass them on. Those are the values we are identifying now and living out in our life experiences and passing them on.

EXAMPLES OF MISSION STATEMENTS

Does the challenge of creating a family mission statement sound impossible because you barely have time to get the meals on the table and the kids bathed and put to bed by the end of each day? Well, try breaking the task down into manageable pieces.

Begin with a personal mission statement. Write down the values and goals that are important to you as an individual and the lessons you've learned in your own life. Following are some examples.

From a newlywed couple on their wedding day:

We desire for God to form us into the image of Christ. We want to be used by Him in this world. We are both aware we only have one short life to live and desire to embrace His work wherever we find it.[17]

From a working mother:

I will seek to balance career and family as best I can since both are important to me.

My home will be a place where I and my family, friends, and guests find joy, comfort, peace, and happiness . . .

I value the rights, freedoms, and responsibilities of our democratic society. I will be a concerned and informed citizen . . .

I will be a self-starting individual who exercises initiative in accomplishing my life's goals . . .

I will always try to keep myself free from addictive and destructive habits . . .

My money will be my servant, not my master . . .

From a businessman:

Succeed at home first.

Seek and merit divine help.

Never compromise with honesty.

Remember the people involved.

Hear both sides before judging.

Obtain counsel of others.

Defend those who are absent.

Be sincere yet decisive.

Develop one new proficiency a year.

Plan tomorrow's work today.

Hustle while you wait.

Maintain a positive attitude.

Keep a sense of humor.

Be orderly in person and in work.

Do not fear mistakes—fear only the absence of creative, constructive, and corrective responses to those mistakes.

Facilitate the success of subordinates.

Listen twice as much as you speak.

Concentrate all abilities and efforts on the task at hand, not worrying about the next job or promotion.[18]

After crafting a personal purpose statement, combine your values with those of your mate to create a family mission statement. Here again, are some samples.

From a young family:

Our goal is to live in harmony by considering each other's needs as more important than our own.[19]

From another young family:

Our purpose as a family is to provide a safe environment for children and grown-ups alike to learn more about loving and serving Jesus through the act of learning how to love and serve each other.[20]

From Edith Schaeffer, author of *What Is a Family?*:

A family is a formation center for human relationships. The family is the place where the deep understanding that people are significant, important, worthwhile, with a purpose in life, should be learned at an early age.[21]

From Billy Graham:

The family should be a closely knit group. The home should be a self-contained shelter of security; a kind of school where life's basic lessons are taught; and a kind of church where God is honored; a place where wholesome recreation and simple pleasures are enjoyed.[22]

Examples from other people can jump-start your own thinking. If you simply don't have time to write your own, copy parts of these that are applicable for your family and adopt them as your own.

CONCLUSION

How vital it is to verbalize who we want to be as a family! As Gloria Gaither warns, ". . . in the final analysis, what we think is most important is what we will choose, no matter what we tell ourselves or other people."[23]

Identifying our mission as a family will help us set our priorities and make the choices that determine how we spend our time and money and shape our families for the future. It gives us a purpose beyond our circumstances, a blueprint plan for what we are building and creating in our family. A family mission simplifies and stabilizes and strengthens the family mobile.

MOBILIZER #1: LIGHTEN UP
The Makings of a Good Marriage

1. First off—don't be mule-headed.
2. Make the most of what ya've got; make the least of what ya've not.
3. Give love by the bushel not by the cupful.
4. Remember—what's good for the goose is good for the gander.
5. Finally, at the end of the day give your troubles to God—He's going to be up all night anyway.[24]

MOBILIZER #2: GUIDELINES TO GOAL-SETTING

- Set aside some time together to talk about your mission and goals.
- Select different categories for goal-setting, such as marriage, parenting, traditions, work, money, faith, education, and physical fitness.
- Make your goals "together goals," for you as a couple and you as a family.
- Set goals that are measurable and attainable.
- Attach a timeline to each goal.
- Set only a limited number of goals.

MOBILIZER #3: SETTING
YOUR OWN MARRIAGE GOALS

How To: "Step By Step"

Step 1: Define Your Purpose

What would you like your marriage to become? What is the general direction toward which you would like your marriage to move? Make a statement about that.

Step 2: Picture the Situation

Imagine your marriage relationship not as it is now, but as you would like it to be. What does it look like? What are you doing? What are the circumstances?

Step 3: State Your Immediate Goals

What things do you have to accomplish now if you are going to move toward your ultimate purpose in your marriage?

Step 4: Act

Pick out one of the goals for your marriage and start moving toward it. Remember: every long journey begins with the first step! And before you act, pray.

Step 5: Act as If . . .

Act as if you have already reached your goal. If you are going to start working toward that first goal, you are going to have to start acting as if you have really reached it.

Step 6: Keep Praying

If you are going to live life with a purpose, then you need to keep seeking God's leading in all this. Yes, you prayed before you acted, but pray also through the whole planning process.

How It Worked for One Couple

The following is a vision statement a couple in their thirties developed and are now using to guide the direction of their marriage. They said their overall goal for their life and marriage was as follows: Love the Lord our God with all our hearts, our souls, and our minds (from Matthew 22:36–40). Specifically, their goals are to demonstrate this love to each other and to others by:

Our Spiritual Well-Being
Serve God wherever he leads us.

Our Marital Well-Being
Be encouragers by (see 1 Thess. 5:11):
Giving the other person the benefit of the doubt.
Believing in each other's dreams.
Affirming and protecting one another.
Being active listeners.
Cherishing and respecting each other.

Our Familial Well-Being
Model Christlike love (see Eph. 5:22, 33).
Uphold our home as a haven.

Our Physical Well-Being
Maintain our bodies through regular physical activity.

Our Mental Well-Being
Share interesting topics that stimulate dialogue.
Take advantage of continuing educational opportunities.

Our Emotional Well-Being
Recognize and acknowledge crisis.
Anticipate stresses and plan accordingly.
Make lifestyle changes as needed to enhance our relationship.

Our Financial Well-Being
Remember that our finances and material possessions have been entrusted to us by God (see Matt. 24:45–46).
Maintain a spirit of giving (see 1 Tim. 6:17–19).

Our Social Well-Being
  Because we as individuals gain energy through reflection,
  introspection, and solitude, we must accept responsibility for our social lives by:
  Developing and maintaining close and meaningful
  relationships.
  Seeking and creating social atmospheres that are comfortable for us.[25]

MOBILIZER #4: CELEBRATE MARRIAGES

Do you belong to a small group of married couples? Why
not celebrate wedding anniversaries as a group? At the couple's
anniversary celebration, you might:

- Serve cake and punch, or similar wedding-type snacks.
- Have the couple describe their courtship.
- Ask the couple to bring their wedding album or a wed-
  ding picture.
- Encourage the couple to reflect out loud about one of
  their wedding vows, especially how it has grown in
  meaning.
- Pray as a group for the couple being honored.

MOBILIZER #5: WHEN THERE'S
NOT ENOUGH TIME OR MONEY

- E-mail each other.
- Meet for lunch, either for fast food or for a picnic in the
  park.

- Tuck a note into each other's work bag or sack lunch.
- Swap "nights out" with another couple and spend your evening alone at home with no kids.
- Put the kids in a Mom's Day Out program and take a day off from work together.
- Find a half-hour to be alone together on either end of the day.

MOBILIZER #6: TRAITS OF A HEALTHY FAMILY

The healthy family . . .

- Communicates and listens
- Affirms and supports each other
- Teaches respect for each other
- Develops a sense of trust
- Has a sense of play and humor
- Exhibits a sense of shared responsibility
- Teaches a sense of right and wrong
- Has a strong sense of family in which rituals and traditions abound
- Has a balance of interaction among members
- Has a shared religious core
- Respects the privacy of one another
- Values service to others
- Fosters table time and conversation
- Shares leisure time
- Admits to and seeks help with problems[26]

MOBILIZER #7: IDENTIFYING
YOUR FAMILY'S VALUES

What does your family stand for? In order to identify your shared values, think about what you share a passion for. What values have been passed down from your parents that you want to pass down to your children? What do you want your family to look like and act like in five years; ten years; as adults together? What values are you instilling by the way you are living now?

As Tim Kimmel puts it in his book *Legacy of Love,* "Your words, your schedule, your choices, your obedience, the way you savor your victories and the way you swallow your defeats all help to define your life. It is this definition that your children rely on most as they seek to chart their own future."[27]

Another way to identify the values you are instilling is to imagine attending your own funeral. What would your family say about you? What would you want to change now so that those remarks would be positive? These questions will help you identify your family values.

MOBILIZER #8: CREATE THE
LEGACY OF FAMILY HISTORY

Families and children both benefit from learning about their heritage. It helps them to know who they are individually and as a family. It helps them know where they are going because they know where they came from. That's why photo albums are so important in families. So are family stories which detail the traits and values that have been part of a family's heritage for generations.

Here are some questions to help you recall your family history:

• What do you know about the generations that preceded you?
• Who is the first person in your family history you know about?
• What do you know about that person?
• Who is a relative that displayed great courage, perseverance, humor, or other outstanding qualities?
• What hardships has your family endured?
• What great fortune has your family experienced?
• Who could you talk to who could help you fill pieces into your family's historical picture?

If you need some help in compiling your family's history through pictures or words, here are some resources:

1. **Creative Memories:** offers supplies, information, ideas, and camaraderie as you learn how to assemble creative keepsake albums (1–800–468–9335).
2. **Memory Makers:** a magazine to support and encourage scrapbook makers with layout suggestions and tips (1–800–366–6465).
3. **Heritage Publishing and Heirlooms:** helps you gather information, write, edit, and publish your family history. The fee is not cheap, but should be well worth it (1414 Allison Drive, Loveland, CO 80538).

MOBILIZER #9: HOW TO WRITE A FAMILY MISSION STATEMENT

Here are some tips for creating a mission statement that summarizes what you hope to accomplish during your years together as a family living under one roof:

Brainstorm

Call a family meeting for brainstorming. The goal is to have fun and treat each other with respect. Point out that God could have selected any combination of people to place within your family, yet he handpicked each one of you. Ask your children why they think God put you all together as a family the way he did. Suggest you brainstorm ten goals he might have for you to accomplish as a family.

Write everything down. No idea should be criticized or dismissed. Don't take yourselves too seriously. Have fun. Be creative. A tip: Take any negative goals ("One of our goals is to fight less") and make them positive ("One goal is to live in harmony with each other").

Now select several ideas to include in your family mission statement. Consider this example: "Our purpose as a family is to love each other and others, to learn life's lessons together, and to honor God."

Celebrate Your Mission Statement

Now that you have a purpose statement, look for ways to celebrate your new goals. Create a family newsletter or certificate that highlights your mission statement. Select a flower or tree that represents some aspect of your mission statement and include it in your backyard landscape. Bake a cake and write the family verse in frosting on the top. Choose a piece of art that symbolizes your mission statement.

Practice Your Mission Statement

Write down twelve activities that put legs to the concepts in your purpose statement. Each week ask one person in your family about what he or she is doing that's in line with the family purpose. Remember, practice makes perfect.[28]

MOBILIZER #10: LOVE YOUR MOTHER-IN-LAW

She may share your personality traits or complement them. You may enjoy a closeness you never had with your own mother, or perhaps you are kind of a wedge between her and her son. Whatever your relationship with her, she is the mother of the man you loved enough to marry. How well do you love her?

Stop for a minute and consider what she brings into your life. Wisdom? Challenge? Fun? Love? Patience? Flexibility? Order?

Now add to this list the characteristics you see in her that your husband shares. How is he like her? How is he different? What have you learned in loving him that could help you love her better?

God doesn't make mistakes. When he brings couples together, whole families are woven together. However you analyze the woman who is your mother-in-law, one fact is certain: She is the mother of the man you love. And in loving her, you are loving him.[29]

MOBILIZER #11: SHARING HOUSEHOLD CHORES

Couples often need to reach agreements about who does what when it comes to household chores. Here are a few tips to help you maintain balance in this area of shared responsibility.

To women:

1. When you need help, ask for it, straight and simple. Don't merely sigh or complain or expect him to read your mind.
2. If you delegate a task, don't redo it after he's done it.
3. Lighten up and have realistic (not perfectionistic) expectations.

To men:

1. Don't expect your wives to be managers of everything. Take some initiative.
2. Don't say you "don't know how." Learn to do the laundry, cook a meal, or run the vacuum.
3. Don't ask her to find your keys or papers or sunglasses.
4. Clean up after yourself. Put your dishes in the dishwasher, your dirty clothes in the laundry, your coat in the closet.

MOBILIZER #12: PARENTING GOALS

Here are two lists of the needs of children. As you think about your own family, which of these matter most to you, and how are you meeting these needs in your children?

What Every Child Needs

- **Security:** Hold-Me-Close Love convinces them they are unconditionally loved.
- **Affirmation:** Crazy-About-Me Love underlines that they are cherished.
- **Belonging:** Fit-Me-Into-the-Family Love communicates their significance and sense of belonging.
- **Discipline:** Give-Me-Limits Love provides the protection of boundaries for life.
- **Guidance:** Show-Me-and-Tell-Me Love gives them what they need to know in life.
- **Respect:** Let-Me-Be-Me Love accepts them for who they are.
- **Play:** Play-With-Me Love allows them to do the work of play.
- **Independence:** Let-Me-Grow-Up Love offers permission and freedom to mature.
- **Hope:** Help-Me-Hope Love conveys an eternal perspective, that there is more to life than just today.[30]

Six Character Traits Every Child Needs

1. **Attachment—Laying the Foundation of Life.** The most basic and important character ability is the ability to form relationships. Children need to learn to need, trust, depend, and have empathy for others.

2. **Responsibility—Developing Self Control.** Your child is born thinking her life is your problem. But part of growing character is helping her to take ownership over her life and to see her life as her problem.

3. **Reality—Living in an Imperfect World.** This deals with the ability of your child to accept the negatives of the real world. His parents and friends will let him down. He will let others down. Parents help their children in the process of dealing with sin, loss, failure,

and evil, not only in themselves, but in others and in the world.

4. **Competence—Developing Gifts and Talents.** Children need training to develop their God-given gifts and talents. They need to develop skill not only in specialty areas such as art, sports, or science, but also in decision making, judgment, and work ethics.

5. **Morality—Making a Conscience.** An internal sense of right and wrong is a growth process in children. Kids' consciences are developed at different ages and stages in life.

6. **Worship—Connecting to God.** Your child has been created in the image of God. Certain tasks foster character development in spiritual growth.[31]

MOBILIZER #13: FINANCIAL GOALS

Most "money problems" within marriages can be traced to difficulties in one of three areas:

1. *Accountability.* . . . Christian financial advisor Larry Burkett explains that the crux of marital finances isn't who writes the checks and balances the checkbook; the important issue is being accountable to each other. . . . Cooperation necessarily involves yielding your personal right in favor of what's best for the marriage. . . . A different accountability problem arises in those marriages where one partner simply takes over the finances or, conversely, refuses to accept responsibility for any financial matters. The result is that one spouse becomes the caretaker while the other is, in effect, the child. . . .

2. *Honesty.* . . . Nurturing trust through consistent honesty is the key to building a solid relationship. When we allow any amount of dishonesty—regarding finances or anything

else—to take root in our lives, we risk the gradual destruction of our marital foundation.

3. Expectations... Depending on their previous experience with finances, such as how money was handled in their childhood home, each partner may bring a different perspective on money.

Overspenders often exhibit a *carpe diem* attitude, looking for personal fulfillment in the accumulation of things. Savers, in contrast, store up their treasures in a search for financial security. . . .

The key to resolving different financial expectations is to come to a mutual understanding that the money we've been given actually belongs to God, and that He will hold us accountable for how we manage His resources.[32]

Tips for Managing Family Finances

Family finances are even more important after children enter a marriage. Children bring added expenses to the family budget, and managing money can become more challenging, especially if one parent has decided to stay home. Here are some suggestions to help you manage your family finances.

1. Discuss money matters. Don't sweep them under the rug.
2. Have both partners be aware of the family finances.
3. Plan goals jointly.
4. Get organized.
5. Take turns paying bills.[33]

Setting Values About Money

Three questions to consider as you think about the value of money in your family:

1. How did you get it?
2. What did you do with it?
3. What did it do to you?

Questions to Ask Each Other

- How has our definition of family changed now that we have children?
- What is our family's overall purpose statement?
- What are the most important values in our family?
- What are our family's top three priorities?
- What qualities do we want each one of our children to have by the time they are adults?
- What can we be doing right now to help our children grow accordingly?
- What traditions that we grew up with would we like to keep?
- What new traditions would we like to add for Christmas, birthdays, or other holidays?
- How do our work responsibilities fit into our family life priorities?
- What attitudes about money do we share? In what ways do we tend to disagree about money?
- What, if anything, would we like to change about our relationships with our extended family?
- In what ways do we want our family to be involved in our community?

Recommended Reading

Is There a Family in the House? Kenneth Chafin
The Financially Confident Woman, Mary Hunt
The Marriage Builder, Lawrence J. Crabb Jr.
Master Your Money, Ron Blue
The Shelter of Each Other: Rebuilding Our Families, Mary Pipher

Six

Hope

REKINDLING HOPE

Where is "happily ever after"?

Paula shifted her weight on the hospital bed in the curtained-off area of the emergency room and tried to remain calm. The ultrasound machine whirred as the technician expertly traced the outline of the baby's form on her tummy, searching for signs of life. "The doctor will be with you in a moment," she gently said to Paula as she left. Paula already knew the horrible truth. Her baby might not make it.

The room became eerily quiet after the technician left. Everything seemed still and lifeless. Was the space within her womb lifeless as well? She looked around and suddenly felt more alone than she'd been in years. She'd left three-year-old Whitney with a neighbor and her husband, Mark, was on his way— supposedly.

Things were not good in their marriage. Mark just didn't seem to care anymore. Sure, he went through the motions: playing with Whitney, bringing home a paycheck, taking up a place at the dinner table. But Paula sensed his heart wasn't in their relationship anymore. He'd rather be at work or with his friends. Anywhere but with her. Even when he was around, he wasn't really *there*.

When she dug deeply into her own heart, she had to admit that her love for him had changed as well. There simply wasn't much warmth and vitality in their relationship anymore. In fact, there was hardly any *life*. She'd hoped the new baby would change things. And now...

The beeper on Mark's pager interrupted him just as he completed a sales call. He borrowed the secretary's phone and called the plant. Paula was in the hospital. Something was wrong with the baby. The dullness in Mark's heart numbed his feelings. Yes, he cared. But the passion and tenderness he once felt for Paula seemed so far away now. His love just didn't flow like it had in the earlier years of their relationship. Having a daughter like Whitney had deepened and stretched his sense of commitment to his family, but the love he'd experienced towards his wife seemed diminished. As he pulled on his coat and headed to the car, the cold night air stung his face. The same kind of freezing winds blew across his heart as well. Was there any life left in his love?

Paula lay still on the hospital bed, waiting. A nurse returned to check on her and said again that the doctor would be in shortly. Paula nodded and gently caressed her belly. *Oh, baby, dear baby,* she whispered as tears filled her eyes. *Please live. You are our only hope.* Closing her eyes, she then began talking to God, for the first time in a long time. *Dear God,* she pleaded, *please save my baby. Please save my marriage. Maybe you are my hope.*

As he pulled into the hospital parking lot, Mark's mind whirred. Marriage was so much *work*. So tedious. Misunderstandings and disagreements mounted up, and rather than trying to tackle the growing mountain of problems, Mark found it easier to avoid any discussions about their relationship altogether. No wonder it was easier to get his needs met elsewhere: around the office, where his boss thought he was awesome; with a coworker who believed in him; at the gym, where he could still show off his body. Paula never oohed and aaahhed over him anymore. And she never seemed satisfied with his fatherly nor his husbandly efforts. He was tired of trying to "fix" their problems.

But what about Whitney? And this unborn baby?

Suddenly his pulse quickened. The baby . . . if something was wrong with the baby, something might be wrong with Paula too. What if this problem threatened her life? He'd never really, *really* considered that, and now the thought frightened him. He pulled into a parking spot, stopped the car, and slumped over the wheel. *Oh, God,* he prayed, *please don't take my baby! Please don't take my wife! Give us a chance....* He didn't even know what he meant by a chance, but oddly, with those words, he recognized a softening in his heart . . . a gentle thawing of his frozen feelings. For the first time in many months, Mark felt concern—maybe even tenderness—for his wife. He climbed out of the car and quickly headed to the emergency room door.

Inside, Paula still bent her head in prayer, and her hands still caressed the baby within her womb. The curtain around her bed rustled and she looked up to see Mark standing beside her. Their eyes met with unspoken questions. While his presence couldn't solve all their struggles, it offered hope in what had seemed to be such a hopeless place in their marriage.

HOPE FOR EVERY MARRIAGE

Mark and Paula's marriage is not unusual. Every year, thousands of couples walk down the aisle at their wedding ceremony with hope in their hearts. But over the next several years, as they face the challenges of life together, especially the challenges with children, something happens to their hope and to their relationship. Their love grows cold, they question their commitment, and they get bogged down with problems or numbness or impatience or frustration. Unfortunately, according to the statistics, more than half of all couples in the United States will throw in the towel and give up because they have lost hope in their marriage relationship.

Every marriage needs hope, especially every marriage with children. Hope greater than their circumstances. Hope greater than the strength they find within themselves. Hope that helps them see the potential of their relationship, even when times are hard.

Misplaced Hope

Where do you turn when your marriage comes to a spot of hopelessness? What do you do in such moments? Where do you find hope? Begin by looking honestly at your marriage and identifying the source of your hope. You may be surprised at what you discover.

> *Marriage isn't to make you happy;*
> *it's to teach you how to love.*

Some of us marry hoping for *intimacy*. We long for a soul mate. We want someone to make us feel important, valued, and worthwhile, but instead we are belittled. We long to be cherished, but we are ignored. Certainly there are some moments of genuine intimacy in our marriage relationship, but the day-to-day challenges of children and bills and busyness and life tend to isolate us in our longings, leaving us feeling alone and unattached.

Some of us marry hoping for *healing*. We hope that what went wrong in our original family will go right in our new family. We seek the stability we missed growing up. From our mate, we pursue the tender or protective parenting we never had. We work to reproduce the best moments of our past while trying to forget the worst. All too often, however, we discover that the one we married brought his or her own sack of unresolved issues to the marriage, a collection of unfulfilled goals or needs which we must now meet. The unconditional love we pursued now becomes dependent upon a list of expectations.

Still others marry hoping for *happiness*. Believing that neither man nor woman was meant to be alone, we seek a mate who will make us happy and fulfill our dream for life's material possessions: two-car garage, minivan, two children (one of each gender), with plenty of money for family vacations to Disneyland. When an illness, unemployment, a miscarriage, a family member's learning disability, or even a momentary cloud of depression shatters our dream, our marriage suffers.

What kind of hope are you looking for in your marriage? What is the source for your lasting hope?

Lasting Hope

Lasting hope is not found in a new baby, in the oohs and aaahhs of af-

Our marriage partnership is eternal.

firmation from each other, or in a perfect family vacation, new furniture, or a new car. Lasting hope is ultimately found in something beyond ourselves and our circumstances.

Let's reexamine the marriage mobile. A couple meets, falls in love, and marries, attaching the heartstrings of their individual lives to each other in a mobile of marriage. Though husband and wife bob and bounce around with the needs and changes of life, the bonds between them continue to grow stronger. When a child comes into the marriage and is added to the mobile, the configuration changes. The new baby weighs the couple down, yet connects and stretches them in new ways. When that stretching discourages the couple, they might begin to wonder where exactly hope is in the midst of this new structure.

Do you find yourself in the above scenario? When you look down at your child, do you feel the heavy weight of responsibility now attached to you—a baby who's hungry every three hours and it's up to you to feed her, a toddler who must be watched constantly or else he might create crayon murals on the walls, an elementary school child who is having trouble at school and depends upon you to discern what he needs and how to help? Do you worry about new clothes for growing children, orthodontists, safety, and college funds? Where is hope?

Look over at your spouse, this mate of your choice, attached to you by marriage. Years ago, you

We are still a work in progress.

stood at an altar and pledged your love and commitment—till death. But he is tired and falls asleep before you have time to process your needs with him. She is distracted by the children and doesn't seem interested in you anymore. A gap grows, and the heartstrings that tie you together stretch even more as you face the transitions of marriage. Where is hope?

You've been looking down and over. The truth is, you're looking in the wrong place.

Look up. Rather than resting in two individuals, attached horizontally through a civil ceremony without eternal meaning, hope for marriage comes when the attachment is to a Source beyond either individual. Hope for marriage—and for every individual—comes when we attach ourselves to a permanent, eternal source of stability and love. It comes in a relationship with God through his Son, Jesus.

Our need for hope. To understand a person's need for God, look first at your own need for hope and where you've been seeking it. Your children can't provide you with the consistent hope you need; they have too many needs themselves. And what about your spouse? Can he or she fill your need for hope? The truth is, we are married to people who are in process. No human, however intimately attached we may be to them, can meet our deepest need for hope because no human can love perfectly.

Happiness in marriage is not an end in itself, but a means toward fulfilling God's purpose for our lives.

— ✳ —

We try to make it a three-way relationship—husband, wife, and God.

Only God can fill the longings of your heart, because only God loves you perfectly. Only he can provide the eternal source of stability from which to hang your marriage.

But a deeper understanding of our need for God comes when we turn the issue around. Instead of looking at the ways we attempt to *get* hope, let's look at our ability to *provide* hope to others in our lives.

When your children approach you with needs day in and day out, you can't always deliver. There's simply not enough of you to meet each request for another glass of juice, a listening ear, a comforting hug. Sometimes you're too busy with other deadlines. Sometimes you can't be there. Sometimes you're just too tired and distracted and running on empty yourself. You reach into your reservoirs of wisdom and patience and realize you have none left to meet your children's needs or solve their problems.

The same is true in your relationship with your spouse. You aren't always loving, always kind, always forgiving, always *for* him or her, as the familiar love verses from the Bible tell you to be. Someone even gave you a framed version of these verses. Every day you walk by it in the hallway and see these words:

> *After having children, my wife and I rededicated our lives to Christ and joined a church and became involved in it.*

    Love is . . .
    Patient and kind . . . not arrogant or rude . . .
    Love does not insist on having its own way.
    Love is not irritable or resentful.
    Love keeps no record of wrongs.
    Love always protects . . . always trusts . . . always hopes . . . always perseveres.

                  FROM 1 CORINTHIANS 13:4–7

You see the word *always* and cringe, because you don't always love in this way. Sometimes you're selfish. Sometimes you're rude. Sometimes you're downright stubborn and insist on your own way.

So where is hope when you fail?

You don't realize that the tough times will deepen your love far more than the good times if you let the Lord work in your marriage.

— x* —

Since becoming parents we pray more together (out of necessity).

— x* —

When I need help in our marriage, I turn to God's Word.

Here's lasting hope. Eventually you realize that you can't find the hope you need in your children or your mate. Neither can you be their hope.

There's a simple reason why this is the case. It's called *sin*. Sin is part of our human nature; we are imperfect people living in an imperfect world. We can't do it right by ourselves. Because God is perfect and can't be in the presence of imperfection, our sin separates us from him—from the very Source that can provide hope for us.

Good news! God loves you and wants to be in relationship with you. So he chose to take care of this sin problem himself by allowing his Son, Jesus, to die on the cross. His death pays for your sins and makes it possible for you to be forgiven for all the imperfect blotches in your life. All you have to do is ask. When you grasp the truth that you can't always deliver or receive the hope needed when you *look down* at your children or *look over* at your spouse, you are ready to *look up*.

When you reach the end of yourself and your ability to be everything for those around you, you turn to God and receive his hope with this simple prayer:

> Dear Jesus, I need hope. When I look down, all I see is the responsibility of my children. They can't provide what I need. I can't provide all they need. When I look over, I see the needs of my mate. I can't find all that I need there. I can't always love him (or her) the way I want to. Their love is imperfect, and so is mine. I believe that you died on the cross for my sins and imperfections. Please come into my life as my Savior. I attach myself to you as the Source of my life.

I hang my life on you and on no other. Please come into my life and begin a relationship with me. Amen.

As we raise our children together, we see God as the source of the strength we need.

We need to get plugged into a good church.

If you prayed that prayer just now as you read it, you can be sure that today you have a new reason to hope! You may not feel so different immediately, but you can start living with the promise that Jesus loves you and that he will help you on a day-to-day basis. You no longer have to wonder where you'll find your hope and strength. In fact, your marriage was designed to be lived in partnership with your mate, with Jesus as your Leader.

WHAT LASTING HOPE BRINGS TO A MARRIAGE

When couples attach themselves to God as the Source of their hope, they begin to change individually, as a couple, and as parents. No longer are they trying so hard to "be everything" for each other, and failing, but rather they are empowered by a process of growing dependency upon God, who enables them to love each other better. As one husband confessed, "For a long time I assumed it was my wife's responsibility to make me happy. Finally, I realized that is not her responsibility. It is my responsibility to turn to God, who is my source for strength every day."

There are several reasons lasting hope brings strength and growth to your marriage.

Internal Reality Affects External Relationships

According to Billy Graham, "Marriage is a divine institution. Society didn't make marriage. It didn't evolve. . . . Marriage was born in the mind of God."[1] Marriage is the earthly model of a heavenly relationship of God's love for us, and when we attach ourselves to God as the Source of hope for our marriages, we are changed from the inside out. As we allow God to love us and to love our spouse through us, we express and experience more of 1 Corinthians 13 love than we can imagine.

This internal reality changes the way we view our external circumstances, including our marriages. Neil Clark Warren explains it this way:

> The world we live in every day, what we call the material world, largely involves the external—that which is outside our skin. If we try to build a great marriage that focuses exclusively on the material world, the foundation will be shallow. But spirituality involves what is inside. It is built around a quest for deeper meaning, for a clearer sense about profound and eternal matters. . . .
>
> It is, then, this moving away from the material world and into the spiritual realm that takes a marriage from the superficial to the profound, from the immediate to the eternal, from two distinct individuals to two who merge into "one flesh." In the process, their relationship becomes stronger, larger, more colorful, and more satisfying.[2]

I need my husband to offer hope, not logic and reason.

— ✳ —

This feeling of imbalance never ends because we are always growing and changing.

— ✳ —

I try to keep my husband's needs ahead of my children's needs in my head and heart.

Lasting Hope Redefines the Needs of Marriage

We've talked about six basic needs of a marriage with children and the ways these needs are recognized and met. But when you put God in the center of the challenge created by each of these needs, our perspective changes. We see the needs of marriage in a whole new way, because God brings us hope, which changes our attitudes and our hearts. Let's look at each of these needs again as we attach ourselves to God and receive his hope in the process.

Just as we are able to love our wives because of God's love for us, so are we able to love our children because of the love we first shared with our spouse. It is very important to have these love relationships in a proper light for a healthy marriage.

— ✳ —

The best part of our marriage is seeing the wonder in our children's eyes as they learns new things about their world.

Balance. In a marriage mobile, a couple is attached to each other by their heartstrings, but when both are attached to God, a new stability is found. Life always brings changes—circumstances change, feelings change, people change. But God never changes. Looking to him for the stable guidelines of life brings balance to a marriage.

Commitment. In a marriage with children, we learn that commitment means working at love, even when we don't feel loving. That work doesn't always come easily or naturally. The Bible describes the first love story on earth between Adam and Eve. When Adam and Eve ate from the tree of knowledge, their eyes were opened to the realities of life. They discovered their marriage was not perfect. They suddenly recognized their lover's faults and shortcomings, and the stresses of work and family life. But as David and Heather Kopp tell us in *Love Stories God Told,* God did not abandon them.

> Marriage was not perfect, but love was still possible, "and that is the hope that echoes down to us through time. . . When the bliss of romance falters, another kind of love promises comfort, forgiveness, healing and hope. . . . In the familiar embrace of our beloved, we hear God exclaim again, 'It is good!' And we find new strength to face our world together."[3]

Interdependence. Interdependency comes when two independent people recognize their dependency on each other. But that dependency is inconsistent and falters as we sometimes pull away from each other and insist on our own way, or we say or do things totally independent of our spouse's needs or feelings. This kind of independent attitude is changed when we recognize our humility or our need for and total dependence upon God. The Bible calls this dependency "abiding in the vine," a vital, life-giving relationship with God that enables us to recognize our need for others, especially our need for interdependency in marriage. As Jesus tells us, "Apart from me, you can do nothing" (John 15:5).

Intimacy. Intimacy is a feeling of closeness that comes from understanding the heart and soul of another. In our discussion of intimacy, we talked about various levels of intimacy sought and experienced by married couples. But God created us first for intimacy with him. Our relationship with God brings the highest and deepest intimacy possible. God assures us that he "has loved us before the beginning of time, has come for us, and now calls us to journey toward him, with him, for the consummation of our love."[4]

This divine intimacy gives us a source of divine love that enables us to experience greater intimacy in our marriage. God ordained sexual intimacy in marriage, and intends for a husband and wife to enjoy their physical relationship like the one described in the Bible's Song of Songs, a love letter intended to inspire intimacy. For instance, here are two examples: "Strengthen me with raisins, refresh me with apples, for I am faint with love. His left arm is under my heard, and his right arm embraces me" (Song of Songs 2:5-6) and "I am my lover's and my lover is mine" (Song of Songs 6:3).

Mission. Mission is the statement of purpose and goals for our marriage and all aspects of it, including family, parenting, budgeting, values, and priorities. Where do these goals come from? When we attach the goal-setting process to God and his

Word in the Bible, we find a divine focus and powerful vision of who we are and what our purpose should be. Ask

What our marriage needs most is the Lord, and guidance through his Word.

yourself: "Why did God put us together in marriage? What does he want us to accomplish as a family?" Your mission verse might become: "As for me and my household, we will serve the LORD" (Joshua 24:15). When, as a couple, your purpose and goals are attached to God, you and your spouse will have a place to keep coming back to as you go through the transitions of life together.

Hope. When the object of our hope becomes God, we attach ourselves to an eternal, unchanging, loving, guiding, personal source of inspiration and strength. When we attach our marriage mobile to God, we hang together with lasting assurance that as a couple we will endure whatever we face. We look forward to the future and eternity, always knowing that the best is yet to come.

Lasting Hope Deepens Intimacy

In general, everything attached to God grows deeper in meaning. This is especially true for the marriage relationship. This deeper intimacy is called spiritual intimacy, defined by H. Norman Wright as "a heart's desire to be close to God and submit to His direction for your lives."[5] The idea of spiritual intimacy is fleshed out in the book *The Spiritually Intimate Marriage,* where Donald R. Harvey describes it as "being able to share your spiritual self, find this reciprocated, and have a sense of union with your mate."[6]

HOW TO DEVELOP SPIRITUAL INTIMACY IN YOUR MARRIAGE

We recognize that a married couple deepens their love and potential for lasting happiness when they process life together spiritually. But how does a couple develop their spiritual intimacy? Here are some ways:

Receive the Gift of Hope Your Children Bring to Your Marriage

Children help us hope. They don't provide hope nor are they the *reason* to hope, but children bring gifts of hope to marriage, which helps a couple persevere through the challenge or times of transition. After all, hope is the ability to see beyond what is to what might be.

Children make us try harder. The very existence of children in a home leads us to try harder at marriage. It's not just about us as a couple; it's about other lives and their future. When we bump and sway with the breezes of life, the fact that we have children causes us to consider our responses and our choices with greater gravity and determination.

> *The longer we've been married, the better it has become. We have grown to understand our likenesses and differences. We are not trying to change each other anymore.*

Children make us more accepting. Pediatric oncologist Diane Komp, who works intensely with children of all ages, writes, "There is something in the beauty of reconciliation possibilities with children that isn't always there with adults. . . . Children force us into confessing our own faults."[7] Children are so quick to give and accept an apology and move on. How much we can learn from them! Their openhanded reception of our inadequacies is a wonderful model of what we can offer each other in marriage and in life.

Learn to Forgive

Marriage experts Les and Leslie Parrott cite unforgiveness as one of the greatest obstacles to marital fulfillment. They write,

At the root of every "record of wrongs" is resentment. The memory of past pain becomes a present injustice as we replay it over in our mind. Yesterday's hurts are nurtured by today's frustration. We soak in it. We don't let it rest. And peace of mind—not to mention peace with our partner—is the price we pay for keeping resentment alive. So why do we do it? . . . The answer is found in false hope. We keep a record of wrongs because we believe we will get our just rewards if we show how bad the other person has been.[8]

Once we realize that we won't satisfy ourselves with vindictiveness and, instead, attach ourselves to God as the Source of our satisfaction, we are freer to forgive others. What have I to gain by holding on to unforgiveness? What have I to lose?

Forgiveness in marriage means turning to God with our woundedness, rather than to our spouse. In his book *Here and Now*, Henri Nouwen reminds us how Jesus responded to wounds inflicted by others. "Let go of your complaints, forgive those who loved you poorly, step over your feelings of being rejected, and have the courage to trust that you won't fall into an abyss of nothingness but into the safe embrace of a God whose love will heal all your wounds."[9]

Forgiveness in marriage also means remembering our own need for forgiveness. No one loves perfectly; everyone needs to be forgiven at some point—probably several times a day! So he cooks your hamburger to well-well done when you prefer it a tiny bit pink. So she forgot to get saltines at the store like you requested as she walked out the door. These are the little irritations that need to be forgiven. And when we don't feel like forgiving quickly, we might stop and think about what we've botched that needs forgiveness. Spiritual intimacy in marriage comes as we learn to let Jesus handle our wounds and to forgive our spouses the way Jesus forgives us.

Go to Church Together

Research shows that couples who attend church together as little as once a month increase their chances of staying married for life. Sociologist Andrew Greely surveyed married people and found that the happiest couples are those who pray together.[10]

One of the most vital tasks for any young family is finding and becoming a part of a church. Talk to your friends about where they attend. Visit several churches and see how comfortable your children are in each. Look for a family-friendly body of believers who understand the needs of growing families and offer programs to address these needs. Join a young family class or a parenting class, or a MOPS and POPS gathering and get to know other families who are adjusting to the transition of being married with children just like you.

Now that we have children, the thing that our marriage needs most is prayer time together. Recently, I was sick and a child was sick. We stopped praying and started whining and were miserable . . . until we realized what we'd done. We started praying again and everything changed, especially our hearts.

Pray Together

Another important part of spiritual intimacy involves prayer. Talking together to God about concerns is a powerful way to grow close to one another in the family as we share each other's burdens. Prayer reminds us that we are not alone in life, but are attached to a great Source who can handle all that comes our way if we ask for help. Many couples pray together in church, but others reach a new depth of intimacy when they pray together at home.

Couples who frequently pray together are twice as likely as those who pray less often to describe their marriages as being highly romantic. And get this—married couples who pray together are ninety percent more likely to report higher satisfaction with their sex lives than couples who don't pray together. Prayer, because of the vulnerability it demands, also draws a couple closer.[11]

HANG IN THERE—IT'S WORTH IT!

When you're dangling from your marriage mobile, little ones hanging from your hands and the winds of transitions howling about you, it's tough to believe that balance will

There was a time I used to cry because I thought our marriage was so awful and my husband was oblivious; but now he is more attentive to doing sweet, unexpected things.

ever be restored. Sometimes your marriage seems to be all out of whack. Or you deny and avoid the reality of the problems you face in your marriage. Other times you just feel numb. But with a firm resolution to make it through these demanding years, your marriage will not only find a new sense of balance, you will be building stronger connections for the future.

When you feel discouraged, talk with those who've been there and survived the bumps of marriage. In our questionnaire to moms and dads of young children, we learned that a majority of couples turn to older Christian friends for advice in marriage. Berkeley psychologist Robert Levenson studied pairs who have been together forty years or more and discovered that these couples are masters at knowing how to soothe one another and prevent each other's distress during conflict. They also evidence a more mellow approach to conflict than younger couples.[12] No wonder we can learn lots from older married couples.

In searching through various descriptions from the marriage mentors around us we've discovered words of wisdom worth sharing on many subjects.

On Commitment

There has never been any doubt about our true love for each other and for God. We have each been confident of our faithfulness to one another, without concern or jealousy, and divorce has never been an option to escape our difficulties.[13]

If we hadn't been committed to God, to the institution of marriage, and to each other, we might not have made it. Such commitment is a good foundation on which romantic love may grow. If you try to base the marriage on emotions, you are in trouble.[14]

On Interdependence

We've allowed each other space, feelings, and ideas that we would discuss and just give each other understanding, supporting one another in ideas and whatever we wanted to do apart. We give each other freedom to be ourselves.[15]

We each take responsibility for our relationship—we don't place it on the other. We compliment each other frequently, say, "I love you" and touch a lot, and work hard to balance doing things together and doing things apart. We promised each other and God to hang in for the long haul, so we pray about problems.[16]

On Intimacy

As a husband, my temper created considerable discord. However, with prayer and discussion, over the years, considerable improvement has been acquired. It has been very important for us to verbally discuss the hurt and embarrassment this problem has created.[17]

As a wife, my lack of showing affection through touching and caressing, and lack of sexual desire have generated many hurt feelings in the middle and later years of our marriage. Through many agonizing discussions and prayer we have struggled with this problem. God has helped us through prayer to be willing to understand each other.... [18]

I knew he loved little white navy beans and ham and cornbread. So I knew that when we needed to make up, I needed
to make navy beans and ham and cornbread. . . . [Looking
back,] I think I would just make more cornbread.[19]

On Mission

Greg and Jackie hereby commit themselves to the following:
(1) to love each other under every circumstance for as long
as they live; (2) to search after meaning and satisfaction together wherever it may be found; (3) to support and encourage each other at every turn of life; (4) to love their kids
generously and personally, and to raise them wisely; (5) to be
involved in serving others, especially the underprivileged; (6)
to respond actively and enthusiastically to the love and guidance of God.[20]

My husband liked having control. As a pleaser and peace-
maker by personality, I seldom if ever confronted him about
his spending on things to make himself feel good. This was
a setup for debt. The road to resolution began by telling myself the truth, about myself and about my husband. After
years of prayer and blind submission, I had to do something
different. Learning to confront firmly and with love has been
extremely difficult, but I'm beginning to see the results.[21]

On Hope

God saved our marriage. When we rededicated our lives to
the Lord, we had divorce papers ready to be signed. We decided to give it one last chance, and since we had tried everything else, we figured we'd give God a chance. What He
did for us was a miracle.[22]

Our spiritual progress during our marriage has been stag-
gered. However, it did not present a problem until thirty
years ago when one of us knew we had come into a much

deeper relationship with Christ, leaving the other mate feeling seriously neglected for some time. When that mate realized through agony, and prayer, that self-control needed to be exercised, and that the other mate was not at the same spiritual high at that same time, and was in fact being neglected, we worked through it with God's help in revealing the truth to us.[23]

In General

If we had any advice to give to couples, it would be just be true to each other. Love each other. I remember one thing I told my wife, "If I did anything wrong, and you want to correct me, don't tell anybody else. Tell me first." And I think she's always done that.[24]

CONCLUSION

Through the years and transitions in life, every marriage experiences changes. Every marriage faces different needs—for balance or commitment or interdependency or intimacy or mission or hope—and in the midst of the wobbliness caused by life's transitions, we discover the importance of attaching our marriage mobile to God.

Once attached to that unchanging, unwavering solid source of love and strength, we begin to realize the great potential in this relationship called marriage. God provides the love and strength we need to hang in there and continue to grow stronger together. He enables us to love each other better. Kenneth Chafin explains it this way:

People who have an unselfish love for one another can work things out. People who really love each other can make mistakes and start over with one another. People who love each other can survive without always getting their own way. People who love each other can adapt themselves to one another. This kind of love at work in the daily experience of a husband and wife can bring an added dimension to all their relationships.[25]

We can find lasting hope when we attach our marriage to God, who shapes us and our marriage for the future. He promises that the "happily ever after" is always ahead of us.

MOBILIZER #1: LIGHTEN UP

Loved the wedding! Invite me to the marriage.

GOD

(A billboard message)

MOBILIZER #2: BIBLICAL PROMISES
TO HANG YOUR MARRIAGE ON

God Ordained Marriage...

The LORD God said, "It is not good for the man to be alone. I will make a helper suitable for him."

GENESIS 2:18

Two Are Better...

Two are better than one, because they have a good return for their work: If one falls down, his friend can help him up. But pity the man who falls and has no one to help him up! Also, if two lie down together, they will keep warm. But how can one keep warm alone?

ECCLESIASTES 4:9–11

Put God in Your Marriage...

Though one may be overpowered, two can defend themselves. A cord of three strands is not quickly broken.

ECCLESIASTES 4:12

Love comes from God.

1 JOHN 4:7

We love because he first loved us.

1 JOHN 4:19

God Inspires Intimacy. . .

This is my lover, this my friend.

SONG OF SONGS 5:16

I belong to my lover, and his desire is for me.

SONG OF SONGS 7:10

God Gives Strength and Stability. . .

The joy of the LORD is your strength.

NEHEMIAH 8:10

Jesus Christ is the same yesterday and today and forever.

HEBREWS 13:8

MOBILIZER #3: DEFINITIONS OF HOPE

Hope is a passion for the possible.

KIERKEGAARD

Hope is the joyous, confident expectation of good.

ANONYMOUS

Hope is the ability to hear the music of the future, and the courage to dance to its music in the present.

PETER KUZMIC OF GORDON CONWELL SEMINARY,
QUOTING A BOSNIAN CHRISTIAN

Hope . . . means a continual looking forward to the eternal world.

C. S. LEWIS

Hope is . . . something as important to us as water is to a fish, as vital as electricity is to a lightbulb, as essential as air is to a jumbo jet.[26]

CHARLES SWINDOLL

I have put my hope in your word.

PSALM 119:114

. . . those who hope in the LORD will renew their strength.

ISAIAH 40:31

The LORD is good to those whose hope is in him, to the one who seeks him.

LAMENTATIONS 3:25

Hope Is . . .

On a trip to London with two other couples we sometimes vacation with, we visited the British Museum, where we discovered an unusual painting called *Hope*. On the background of this canvas were the familiar outlines of the continents and oceans of planet Earth. In the foreground was a beautiful woman seated at a harp. Nearly all of the harp's strings dangled helplessly from the top of the harp or lay uselessly on the lap of the woman's dress. Only one string remained taut. One of our friends commented on how little of the harp was still intact and said, "I wonder why they call the painting *Hope?*" The answer was clear to me. Hope is the song of a broken instrument. It is the plucking of that one string and knowing that you can still have music. Hope is what empowers us to draw on our reservoir of determination and make a commitment to improve our circumstances. Hope transforms. That's why love always hopes.[27]

MOBILIZER #4: WHEN HUSBAND AND WIFE ARE BOTH BELIEVERS...

Encourage Spiritual Intimacy

For a couple to have spiritual intimacy, they need shared beliefs as to who Jesus is and what the basic tenets of the Christian faith are.... A wonderful way to encourage spiritual intimacy is to share the history of your spiritual life. Use the following questions to discover more about your partner's faith.

1. What did your parents believe about God, Jesus, church, prayer, the Bible?
2. Where did you first learn about God? About Jesus? About the Holy Spirit? At what age?
3. What questions did you have as a child or teen about your faith? Who gave you any answers?
4. Did you memorize any Scripture as a child? Do you remember any now?
5. As a child, if you could have asked God any questions, what would they have been?
6. If you could ask God any questions now, what would they be?
7. Did anyone disappoint you spiritually as a child? If so, how has that impacted you as an adult?
8. When you went through difficult times as a child or teen, how did that affect your faith?

9. What has been the greatest spiritual experience of your life?

Pray Together

Praying together is perhaps the strongest knot that binds a couple. In his book *To Understand Each Other,* Paul Tournier writes:

> Happy are the couples who do recognize and understand that their happiness is a gift of God, who can kneel together to express their thanks not only for the love which he has put in their hearts, the children he has given them or all of life's joys, but also for the progress in their marriage which he brings about through the hard school of mutual understanding.[29]

Praying together may feel uncomfortable in the beginning. Here are some tips to get you started, minimizing self-consciousness and aiming you toward God-consciousness.

1. Set aside time together, possibly first thing in the morning or on the phone during the children's nap time. Try a date time once a week or on Sunday evenings or while taking a walk or driving in the car together. Whatever works for you. Just do it.
2. Read Scripture together. Try the Psalms. Share favorite passages and talk about how they have touched your life.
3. Get a book of prayers and pray them together.
4. Make a list of prayer requests.
5. Talk about how God has answered prayers in your past.
6. Take a few moments for silent prayer.
7. Pray out loud together for each other, for your marriage, for your children.

Help Each Other Grow Spiritually
Answer these questions together:

- You could help me grow in my faith by _____.
- I feel most comfortable praying with you when _____.
- We could grow together in our faith if _____.
- We could serve God together by _____.
- We could glorify God in our marriage by _____.

MOBILIZER #5: WHEN YOUR
SPOUSE DOESN'T BELIEVE...

Making Your Marriage Work ... When a
Spouse Doesn't Believe

Expect to be happy. Don't expect to be miserable and have insurmountable problems because your spouse is not a believer. We get out of life what we put into it and expect from it.

Expect your spouse to be unreasonable. To the unbeliever, the Bible is no better guidebook for living than any other how-to book. Your spouse probably will enjoy going to the movies more than going to church. Sin is not an issue, and your godliness may be threatening, convicting, and confusing.

Expect problems as part of your life. You may have a tendency to idealize Christian marriages and blame many normal problems on the fact that your spouse is not a believer. The truth is, many problems you face are common to all marriages and are not solely due to the fact that your spouse is not a Christian.

Look for positives. Look for positive character and personality assets in your spouse. What qualities attracted you to each other in the first place? In what ways is your spouse growing? What are some of the things your spouse does that please you?

Be genuine. Act our your faith with sincerity and conviction. What you do or do not do will affect your spouse's opinion of what a Christian should be.

Be loyal. Don't advertise the fact that your spouse is not a believer. Don't speak unkindly of your spouse; put his or her best foot forward when talking about your spouse. Besides, the way you talk about your spouse reflects on you.

Put God first. There will be times you have to choose between God and your spouse. In all things, Christians are commanded to put God first, but ask yourself, can you please your spouse without detracting from Christianity? And remember, there is a difference between self-righteousness and the righteousness of God.

Rely on the character of God. Ultimately, everything any Christian does must be viewed in the light of the character of God. Too often we look at our circumstances instead of at our Lord. But nothing will happen to us that God does not permit.[30]

Feelings Your Unbelieving Spouse May Feel

- Jealousy
- Hurt and rejection
- Pressure
- Uneasiness
- Emotional separation
- Indifference
- Challenge
- Fear
- Reluctance
- Grief
- Anger
- Being used
- Resentment
- Hostility[31]

MOBILIZER #6: FAITH THAT FREES (INSTEAD OF CONTROLS) A MARRIAGE

The Christian faith is meant to be liberating. But sometimes we use it merely as a means of control. When that happens, faith ceases to be biblical and instead becomes a destructive mix of misplaced zeal, cultural chauvinism, and self-serving assertiveness.

We've probably all seen that kind of "religion" at work in a marriage, though it's sometimes more subtle than we realize. For example: A husband may claim Christian authority as head of his house not so much to apply God's will there, but to gain what he desires for his own benefit. A wife may claim the priority of "God's work" as she makes an endless round of church meetings and neglects her household.

The issue may be as minor as the length of a child's hair; in the sixties, both young and old invoked the Bible to "prove" the rightness of their positions. But conflicts often revolve around much larger issues that can generate pervasive tensions in a marriage. Consider these:

1. Choice of church
2. Doctrinal differences
3. Private devotions
4. Church attendance

Whatever the conflict over spiritual matters, if each issue is faced together with prayer for wisdom and toleration, God can grant you a new and shared conviction, or the grace to "agree to disagree." The result will be a spiritual vitality that liberates your marriage and offers a compelling example of godly maturity to your children.[32]

MOBILIZER #7: STANDING BEFORE JESUS

One day we will each stand before Jesus and give an account of how well we loved

- our friends,
- our family,
- our children,
- people we don't even know,
- and our husband or wife.

As you picture yourself giving an account of your support of your spouse, consider:

- To love is to respect.
- To love is to honor.
- To love is to offer tender affection.
- To love is to choose commitment—over and over and over and over again.
- To love is to show kindness and mercy.
- To love is to forgive.
- To love is to invest.
- Love is expressed in word, action, belief, and participation.

As you love your spouse, consider standing before Jesus and giving an account as to how you invested in each other's gifts for the kingdom of Jesus.

- How can you offer the pillar support of your love?
- How will you move aside, allowing for growth?
- How might you take on tasks, freeing another for service?
- How can you mirror giftedness of another, clarifying an offering?

One day we will stand before Jesus and give account for how well we have loved that one we have partnered with in these days on earth.

Love now with that end in mind.[33]

MOBILIZER #8: PHOTO MEMORIES

You get hope for the future by remembering blessings of your past. Many couples surround themselves with photographic reminders of their past blessings, which kindle their love. For instance, keep a really good picture of your spouse in a place where you will see it often, at work or on your desk at home. Here's one woman's story of how photos strengthened her marriage in a different way:

> My mother recalls a time in her marriage when outside pressures were putting a strain on her relationship with my father. About this time, while cleaning out a drawer, she uncovered a cache of pictures taken during the early years of their marriage. One of the pictures in particular tugged on her heartstrings and filled her with remembered joy.
>
> The picture may not seem like much to most. It's a small black and white, poorly composed, faintly out of focus, and faded with age. In it, my dad is sitting on a couch in my grandmother's home. The sleeves on his white dress shirt are

rolled up, his tie is crooked, and his eyeglasses are filled with glare where the camera caught him by surprise. In his arms relaxes one of my sisters, a chubby toddler wearing saddle oxfords and sucking her fingers.

What's special about the photo is the period of time it represents—a span of time, my mother recalls, when babies were little and love was good and life was filled with promise. Several decades later, finding that photo in a forgotten box, my mother was reminded of how much in love she and my dad had been and have been throughout their marriage. For her that day, in the face of external pressures and challenges, the depth of her love for my father was rekindled and renewed.[34]

MOBILIZER #9: LOVE IS . . .

Love is at the heart of every other Christian virtue. Thus, for example, justice without love is legalism; faith without love is ideology; hope without love is self-centeredness; forgiveness without love is self-abasement; fortitude without love is recklessness; generosity without love is extravagance; care without love is mere duty; fidelity without love is servitude. Every virtue is an expression of love. No virtue is really a virtue unless it is permeated, or informed, by love.[35]

MOBILZER #10: GROW TOWARD YOUR GOLDEN WEDDING ANNIVERSARY

On the Eve of Their Golden Wedding Anniversary

"Our Golden Wedding Day draws near," the husband said.

The elderly woman, smiling, raised her head,

"Will you write me a poem as you used to do?
That's the gift I'd like most from you!"

The old man, agreeing, limped from the room,
Went out on the porch in the twilight's gloom,
Leaned on the railing and reminisced:
"Often we sat here, shared hope, and kissed.

"Dear Lord, how the years have hurried by—
Those memories of youth make an old man sigh!
Now we grow weary and bent and gray,
What clever words can I possibly say

"To show that I love her just as much
As I did when her cheeks were soft to my touch,
When her eyes were bright and her lips were warm,
And we happily walked with her hand on my arm!"

So the husband stood while the evening breeze
Echoed his sigh through the nearby trees
Till the joys they had shared in days long past
Merged into thoughts he could voice at last.

And he went inside and got paper and pen;
Sat down at the kitchen table and then
Carefully wrote what his wife had desired:
A gift as "golden" as a love inspired.

"Sweetheart, dear wife, my closest friend,
With you my days begin and end.
Though time has stolen strength and youth,

It cannot change this shining truth:
Our love has lasted all these years
While hardships came and sorrow's tears.
We've met each test and gotten by,
And I will love you till I die!
We are not rich in worldly wealth
But we own nothing gained by stealth,
And you remain my greatest treasure,
My source of pride and quiet pleasure.
I wish you all the happiness
With which two loving hearts are blessed;
You were, and are, my choice for life,
My girl, my lady, my sweet wife!"

The poem finished, the husband arose,
Went into the room where his good wife dozed
And tenderly kissing her nodding head,
"Wake up, 'sleeping beauty,' and come to bed!"[36]

Questions to Ask Each Other

- In our own words, what is hope?
- What do we put our hope in? A good vacation? An evening out together? What is the object of our hope?
- Where are we in our understanding of God, who is our hope?
- What does spiritual intimacy look like in our relationship with each other?
- How can we deepen our spiritual intimacy?
- How do our children contribute to our hope?
- In what ways do we need to apply the concept of hope by choosing to forgive each other?
- How satisfying is our worship together? How can we improve its meaning in our lives?

Recommended Reading

A Daily Marriage Builder for Couples, Fred and Florence
  Littauer
Becoming Soul Mates, Les and Leslie Parrott
Beloved Unbeliever, Jo Berry
Just As I Am, Billy Graham
Lord, I Wish My Husband Would Pray with Me, Larry
  Keefauver
Praying the Bible for Your Marriage, David and Heather Kopp
Quiet Times for Couples, H. Norman Wright
Secrets of a Lasting Marriage, H. Norman Wright
The Couples Devotional Bible
The Spiritually Intimate Marriage, Don Harvey
The Triumphant Marriage, Neil Clark Warren, Ph.D.
Two-Part Harmony—A Devotional for Couples, Patrick Morley
Unbelieving Husbands and the Wives Who Love Them, Michael
  Fanstone

Best Advice About Marriage

We asked, "What is the best advice someone has given you about your marriage?"

— ✱ —

Husbands said ...

Have children.

Love is an action, not a feeling.

Always tell the truth, but tell it in love.

Become a student of your wife.

A marriage is not 50/50; it's both spouses giving 100 percent.

Have a vision for who your wife is becoming.

Show your children you love each other.

Learn to say, "I'm sorry."

Don't sweat the small stuff.

Wives said ...

Marriage isn't to make you happy; it's to teach you how to love.

Don't put your marriage on hold while raising kids.

Remember that you're on the same team.

Don't complain about your spouse to others.

Don't major in the minors.

Don't let little things grow into big things.

Don't expect perfection.

Love...

Love never gives up.

Love cares more for others than for self.

Love doesn't want what it doesn't have.

Love doesn't strut,

Doesn't have a swelled head,

Doesn't force itself on others,

Isn't always "me first,"

Doesn't fly off the handle,

Doesn't keep score of the sins of others,

Doesn't revel when others grovel,

Takes pleasure in the flowering of truth,

Puts up with anything,

Trusts God always,

Always looks for the best,

Never looks back,

But keeps going to the end.

Love never dies.

1 CORINTHIANS 13 (THE MESSAGE)

The MOPS Story

I t was a Tuesday morning, at about 9:30. They had each faced spilled cereal, tangled hair, and a few had even been forced to change their outfits due to last-minute baby throw-up on a shoulder or lap. They had driven, or pushed strollers, to the church and had dropped their little ones off in the nursery. They had made it!

And now they sat, knees almost touching, in the circle of children's chairs from the Sunday school room. Hands held cups of hot coffee and doughnuts in utter freedom because this treat did not have to be shared with a child's sticky fingers. Mouths moved in eager, uninterrupted conversations. Eyes sparkled with enthusiasm. Hearts stirred with understanding. Needs were met.

That morning, in 1973, was the first morning of MOPS, or Mothers of Preschoolers. From its humble beginnings in a church in Wheat Ridge, Colorado, with only a handful of moms, MOPS International now charters MOPS groups in approximately 2,500 churches and parachurch organizations in all fifty of the United States, Canada, and eleven other countries. Groups meet during the day, in the evening, even on weekends.

More than 100,000 moms are touched by a local MOPS group and are encouraged through the media arms of MOPS: *MomSense* radio and newsletter, MOPS' Web site, and publications such as this book. MOPS groups meet the unique needs of mothers of preschoolers in a variety of settings, including urban, suburban, rural, international, and groups specifically geared to teen moms. Mission MOPS provides funds for organizations that need financial assistance for MOPS group leadership training and chartering.

MOPS grew out of a desire to meet the needs of every mother of preschoolers. Today, when a mom enters a MOPS meeting, she is greeted by a friendly face and escorted to MOP-PETS, where her children enjoy their special part of the MOPS program. In MOPPETS, children from infancy through kindergarten experience a caring environment while they learn, sing, play and make crafts.

Once her children are settled, the MOPS mom joins a program tailor-made to meet her needs. She can grab something good to eat and not have to share it! She can finish a sentence and not have to speak in Children-ese!

The program typically begins with a brief lesson taught by an older mom who's been through the challenging early years of mothering and who can share from her experience and from the truths taught in the Bible. Then the women move into small discussion groups where there are no "wrong answers" and each mom is free to share her joys and struggles with other moms who truly understand her feelings. In these moments, long-lasting friendships are often made on the common ground of finally being understood.

From here, the women participate in a craft or other creative activity. For moms who are often frustrated by the impossibility of completing anything in their unpredictable days, this activity is deeply satisfying. It provides a sense of accomplishment and growth for many moms.

Because moms of preschoolers themselves lead MOPS, the program also offers women a chance to develop their leadership skills and other talents. It takes organization, up-front abilities, financial management, creativity, and management skills to run a MOPS program successfully.

By the time they finish the MOPS meeting and pick up their children, the moms feel refreshed and better able to mother. MOPS helps them recognize that moms have needs too! And when they take the time to meet those needs, they find they are more effective in meeting the needs of their families. This is how one mom described MOPS:

"MOPS means I am able to share the joys, frustrations and insecurities of being a mom. Our meetings provide the opportunity to hear someone else say, 'I was up all night' or 'They're driving me crazy!' or 'He doesn't understand.' While listening to others, I may discover a fresh idea or a new perspective that helps me tackle the job of parenting, home management, or being a good wife. It's important to feel normal and not alone. Burdens are lifted when the woman next to me says, 'I know exactly how you feel.' MOPS is a place for my children to interact with peers while I savor some uninterrupted conversation.

"I was not a Christian when I began attending MOPS. Over the past year I have experienced tremendous spiritual growth and I know that MOPS is a contributor to that growth. Now, fellowship with other Christian women is an integral reason for me to attend. I thank the Lord for bringing me and my children to MOPS."

The MOPS program also enables moms to reach out and help other moms, fulfilling not only a need to belong and be understood but a need to help others. To receive information such as how to join a MOPS group, or how to receive other MOPS resources such as *MOMSense* newsletter, call or write the MOPS International office.✶

MOPS International
P.O. Box 102200
Denver, CO 80250–2200
Phone 1–800–929–1287
E-mail: Info@MOPS.org
Web Site: www.MOPS.org

To learn how to start a MOPS group,
call 1–888–910-MOPS.
For information on MOPShop products,
call 1–888–545–4040.

Notes

INTRODUCTION

1. Edith Schaeffer, *What Is a Family?* (Old Tappan, NJ: Revell, 1975), 22.

EPIGRAPH

1. Angela S. Cain, "The Gift," *Welcome Home* (February 1999): 12. Used by permission.

CHAPTER ONE

1. Carla Barnhill, "The Wonder of the First Year," *Christian Parenting Today* (November/December 1998): 32.

2. Linda Burton, "Married Love: A Fond Salute," *Welcome Home* (December 1998): 7–8. Linda Burton is coauthor of *What's a Smart Woman Like You Doing at Home?* (www.mah.org).

3. "A Lens on Matrimony," *U.S. News & World Report* (February 21, 1994): 68–69.

4. Dr. Richard E. Matteson and Janis Long Harris, *What If I Married the Wrong Person?* (Minneapolis, MN: Bethany House, 1996), 106.

5. "The Seven Ages of the Married Cold," *The Saturday Evening Post.* (Note: This quote was typed into a personal letter to the author on June 15, 1988, citing only the name of the periodical from which it was taken.)

6. Frank Minirth et al., *Passages of Marriage* (Nashville, TN: Nelson Publishers, 1991), 8.

7. Minirth et al., *Passages of Marriage,* 9.

8. Anna B. Mow, "The Discipline of Love," *Decision* (June 1998): 13.

9. Elizabeth Cody Newenhuyse, "Are We Still in Love?" *The Christian Reader.* (Note: This is an old issue of *The Christian Reader,*

date unknown. We have this note in the article itself: "Adapted from the forthcoming book *Strong Marriages, Secret Questions*. Used with permission of Lion Publishing Company. ©1990 by Elizabeth Cody Newenhuyse.")

10. Roberta Temes, "New Rules for Marital Unhappiness?" *Psychology Today* (May 1981). (Note: This quote came from a photocopied page found in the author's files, with no page number cited.)

11. "Marriage Seasons," *Dads & Moms* (February 1985). Adapted from H. Norman Wright, *Seasons of a Marriage* (Ventura, CA: Regal, 1982). (Note: *Dad & Moms* is a newsletter without page numbering.)

12. William and Nancie Carmichael, *601 Quotes About Marriage & Family* (Wheaton, IL: Tyndale House, 1998), 73.

13. Dale Evans Rogers as quoted in Carmichael, *601 Quotes About Marriage & Family*, 78.

14. Greg and Erin Smalley, "How Children Change a Marriage," *ParentLife:* 46. (Note: This quote was taken from a photocopied page found in the author's files, with no issue or date cited.)

15. Adapted from Martha Manning, *Chasing Grace* (San Francisco: HarperCollins, 1996), 139-40. Reprinted by permission.

16. Adapted from Rob Parsons, *The 60-Minute Marriage Builder*. Used by permission of Broadman and Holman Publishers.

17. Adapted from Willard F. Harley Jr., *The Four Gifts of Love* (Grand Rapids, MI: Revell, 1998), 44–50.

18. Adapted from James Dobson, "The Marriage Killers," *Focus on the Family* (February 1993): 7.

19. Tom Mullen as quoted in Carmichael, *601 Quotes About Marriage & Family*, 10.

20. Mignon McLaughlin as quoted in Anne Ortlund, *Building a Great Marriage* (Old Tappan, NJ: Revell, 1985), 163.

21. Lillian Hellman as quoted in Ortlund, *Building a Great Marriage*, 179.

22. Anne Morrow Lindbergh as quoted in Carmichael, *601 Quotes About Marriage & Family*, 23.

CHAPTER TWO

1. Joy Jordan-Lake, *Grit and Grace* (Wheaton, IL: Harold Shaw, 1997), 51.

2. Carol Kuykendall, *A Mother's Footprints of Faith* (Grand Rapids, MI: Zondervan, 1997), 57.

3. Elizabeth Sherrill, "The Power of a Promise," *Guideposts* (August 1998): 3.

4. Anna B. Mow, "The Discipline of Love," *Decision* (June 1998): 13.

5. Dr. James Dobson, *Love for a Lifetime* (Sisters, OR: Multnomah Press, 1993), 30.

6. Tim Kimmel, "How Would You Define 'Love'?" *Real Family Life* (September/October 1998): 15.

7. Philip Yancey, "My Legs Ache, But We Made It," *Christianity Today* (April 1996): 104.

8. John T. Gossett as quoted in Anne Gottlieb, "The Secret Strength of Happy Marriages," *McCall's* (December 1990): 95–96.

9. C. S. Lewis, *Mere Christianity* (Westwood, NJ: Barbour and Company, 1952), 92.

10. Mother Teresa as quoted in Les and Leslie Parrott, *Love Is . . .* (Grand Rapids, MI: Zondervan, 1999), 14. Used by permission.

11. Henri J. M. Nouwen, *Here and Now* (New York, NY: Crossroad, 1994), 78.

12. Gary Smalley, "What Each Spouse Needs," *Decision* (April 1996): 17.

13. Nicole Wise, "Best Things to Do for Your Marriage," *Redbook* (October 1997): 139.

14. Philip Yancey as quoted in William and Nancie Carmichael, *601 Quotes About Marriage & Family* (Wheaton, IL: Tyndale House, 1998), 81.

15. John Rosemond as quoted in Wise, "Best Things to Do for Your Marriage," 139.

16. Gary Kinnaman, *Learning to Love the One You Marry* (Ann Arbor, MI: Servant), 16.

17. Harville Hendrix, Ph.D., *Getting the Love You Want* (New York, NY: HarperPerennial, 1988), xiii, xiv.

18. Dr. James Dobson, *Love Must Be Tough* (Waco, TX: Word, 1983), 30–37, 41–50.

19. Neil Clark Warren, Ph.D., *Forever My Love*, (Wheaton, IL: Tyndale House, 1998). All rights reserved. International copyright secured. Used by permission.

20. Janis Abrahms Spring as quoted in Beth Levine, "Crisis-Proof Your Marriage," *Readers Digest* (October 1998): 48.

21. Gary D. Chapman, "Serving the One You Love," *Decision* (June 1998): 17.

22. Parrott, *Love Is . . .* , 24.

23. Vicki Huffman, "Now and Forever," *Virtue* (March/April 1997): 52.

24. Dobson, *Love for a Lifetime*, 113.

25. Anne Ortlund, *Building a Great Marriage* (Old Tappan, NJ: Revell, 1985), 180.

26. Ortlund, *Building a Great Marriage*, 180–82.

27. Warren, *Forever My Love*.

28. Ortlund, *Building a Great Marriage*, 82–83.

29. Taken from *The Baptist Challenge*. (Note: This quote was typed on a scrap of paper found in the author's files, with only the name of the source cited.)

30. Adapted from Ruth Haley Barton, "You're Still the One—Strategies for Safeguarding Your Marriage," *Today's Christian Woman* (November/December 1998): 63–67.

31. Ruth Bell Graham. "Train Our Love," *Decision* (February 1998): 39. Used by permission.

CHAPTER THREE

1. Kathleen Hadley, "Labours of Love," *Tatler* (May 1995).

2. Toni Vogt, *Prism Weight Loss Program Curriculum One* (1990): iii–iv.

3. H. Norman Wright, *Seasons of Marriage* (Ventura, CA: Regal, 1982), 41.

4. Melinda Marshall, "Why'd I Marry Him, Anyway?" *Ladies' Home Journal* (November 1998): 150.

5. Joyce Brothers as quoted in Ken Levine, "How Well Do You Know Your Spouse?" *Reader's Digest* (September 1987): 130.

6. Kenneth Chafin, *Is There a Family in the House?* (Waco, TX: Word, 1978), 57. Used by permission.

7. Ruth Senter, *Have We Really Come a Long Way?* (Minneapolis, MN: Bethany House, 1997), 22.

8. Danielle Crittenden, "The Argument Against Equal Marriage," *Ladies' Home Journal* (February 1999): 76.

9. Dr. Ed Wheat, *Love Life for Every Married Couple* (Grand Rapids, MI: Zondervan, 1980), 30.

10. Annie Gottlieb, "The Secret Strength of Happy Marriages," *McCall's* (December 1990): 134.

11. Chafin, *Is There a Family in the House?* 59.

12. Annie Chapman as quoted in Betty Malz, *Making Your Husband Feel Loved* (Lake Mary, FL: Creation House, 1997), 35–36.

13. Jim and Jeri White, "How to Keep the Weeds Away," *Discipleship Journal* (Issue Fourteen 1983): 25.

14. Elizabeth Cody Newenhuyse, "Are We Still in Love?" *The Christian Reader*, 16. (See note about this source in chapter 1 endnotes.)

15. Poem as submitted from Ulrich Schaffer, *A Growing Love: Meditations on Marriage and Commitment* (New York, NY: Harper & Row, 1977), 53. Used by permission.

16. Gary Kinnaman, *Learning to Love the One You Marry* (Ann Arbor, MI: Servant, 1997), 41.

17. Joey O'Connor, *Women Are Always Right & Men Are Never Wrong* (Nashville, TN: Word, 1998), 233–34.

18. Roy Croft, *Leaves of Gold*, edited by Clyde Lytle (Williamsport, PA: Coslett, 1938), 80.

19. Karen Scalf Linamen, *Pillow Talk: The Intimate Marriage from A to Z* (Grand Rapids, MI: Revell, a division of Baker Book House, 1996), 102–3.

20. John Trent, "Leaving Before Cleaving," in *Parents Resource Bible* (Wheaton, IL: Tyndale, 1995), 5. Used by permission.

21. Trent, "Leaving Before Cleaving," 5. Used by permission.

CHAPTER FOUR

1. Bill and Lynne Hybels, *Fit to Be Tied* (Grand Rapids, MI: Zondervan, 1992).

2. Elisa Morgan and Carol Kuykendall, *What Every Mom Needs* (Grand Rapids, MI: Zondervan, 1995), 78.

3. Adapted from H. Norman Wright, *The Secrets of a Lasting Marriage* (Ventura, CA: Regal, 1995), 153. Used by permission.

4. John T. Gossett as quoted in Annie Gottlieb, "The Secret Strength of Happy Marriages," *McCall's* (December 1990): 134–35.

5. Dr. James Dobson, *Love for a Lifetime* (Sisters, OR: Multnomah Press, 1993), 32.

6. Karen Scalf Linamen, *Pillow Talk: The Intimate Marriage from A to Z* (Grand Rapids, MI: Revell, a division of Baker Book House, 1996), 61. Used by permission.

7. Brent Curtis and John Eldredge, *The Sacred Romance* (Nashville, TN: Nelson, Inc., 1997), 89.

8. Debbie Anway, "Comfortable Love." E-mail to author, November 13, 1998. Used by permission.

9. Becky Freeman, *Marriage 911* (Nashville, TN: Broadman & Holman, 1996), 32.

10. Neil Clark Warren, Ph.D., *Forever My Love* (Wheaton, IL: Tyndale House, 1998). All rights reserved. International copyright secured. Used by permission.

11. Dennis Rainey in Mike Yorky and Sandra P. Aldrich, *The Christian Mom's Answer Book* (Colorado Springs, CO: Chariot Victor, 1998), 25.

12. Nancy Vazquez, "Falling in Love with a Married Man," *Welcome Home* (February 1998): 6.

13. David and Claudia Arp, *Love Life for Parents* (Grand Rapids, MI: Zondervan, 1998), 97. Used by permission.

14. Joyce Maynard, "Life Without Father," *McCall's* (August 1984): 78.

15. Erma Bombeck, "Together's Better," *Reader's Digest* (December 1993): 62–63.

16. Naomi Levy, "Change Your Life . . . Take a Day of Rest," *Parade* (October 11, 1998): 12.

17. Levy, "Change Your Life . . . Take a Day of Rest."

18. Luciano de Cresenzo as quoted in Les and Leslie Parrott, *Love is. . .* (Grand Rapids, MI: Zondervan, 1999), 71. Used by permission.

19. Walter Trobisch, *I Loved a Girl* (New York, NY: Chapel Books, 1965), 26.

20. Gary Smalley and John Trent, *The Language of Love* (Colorado Springs, CO: Focus on the Family, 1988), 77.

21. Clifford Notarius as quoted in Beth Levine, "Crisis-Proof Your Marriage," *Reader's Digest* (October 1998): 47–48.

22. Adapted from Les and Leslie Parrott, *Bring Home the Joy* (Grand Rapids, MI: Zondervan, 1998), 130–37.

23. Linamen, *Pillow Talk,* 205.

24. Kenneth Chafin, *Is There a Family in the House?* (Waco, TX: Word, 1978), 58–59. Used by permission.

25. John Trent, Ph.D., *Love for All Seasons* (Chicago, IL: Moody Press, 1996), 134–35.

26. Anne Ortlund, *Building a Great Marriage* (Old Tappan, NJ: Revell, 1985), 69.

27. Anna Roufos, "LHJ Solutions: Time-Tested Tips and Tricks," *Ladies' Home Journal* (November 1998): 77.

28. Jim and Jeri White, "How to Keep the Weeds Away," *Discipleship Journal* (Issue Fourteen 1983): 26.

29. Adapted from Arp, *Love Life for Parents,* 36–42. Used by permission.

30. Arp, *Love Life for Parents,* 138.

31. Adapted from Neil Clark Warren, Ph.D., *Learning to Live with the Love of Your Life and Loving It,* previously titled *The Triumphant Marriage* (Colorado Springs, CO: Focus on the Family, 1995), 113–16. All rights reserved. International copyright secured. Used by permission.

32. Charles R. Swindoll, "True Lovers Fight Fair," *Smart Families Magazine* (Fall 1998): 8.

33. Adapted from Parrott, *Bring Home the Joy,* 164–67. (Taken from chapter 10, "Negotiate a Mutually Satisfying Sexual Relationship" by Dr. Neil Clark Warren, adapted from his book, *The Triumphant Marriage.*)

34. Linamen, *Pillow Talk,* 100.

35. Adapted from Arp, *Love Life for Parents,* 113–19.

36. John Powell S. J., *Unconditional Love* (Allen, TX: Angus Communicating, 1978), 66-68.

CHAPTER FIVE

1. Kenneth Chafin, *Is There a Family in the House?* (Waco, TX: Word, 1978), 18. Used by permission.

2. Neil Clark Warren, Ph.D., *Forever My Love* (Wheaton, IL: Tyndale House Publishers, 1998). All rights reserved. International copyright secured. Used by permission.

3. Antoine de Saint Exupery as quoted in Les and Leslie Parrott, *Love Is …* (Grand Rapids, MI: Zondervan, 1999), 10. Used by permission.

4. Stephen R. Covey, *The Seven Habits of Highly Effective People* (New York, NY: Simon & Schuster, 1989), 98.

5. Henri J. M. Nouwen, *Here and Now* (New York, NY: Crossroad Publishing, 1994), 68.

6. Warren, *Forever My Love.*

7. Warren, *Forever My Love.*

8. Warren, *Forever My Love.*

9. Neil Clark Warren, Ph.D., *Learning to Live with the Love of Your Life and Loving It,* previously titled *The Triumphant Marriage* (Colorado Springs, CO: Focus on the Family, 1995), 141. All rights reserved. International copyright secured. Used by permission.

10. Dr. Henry Cloud and Dr. John Townsend, *Raising Great Kids* (Grand Rapids, MI: Zondervan, 1999), 25.

11. James Dobson, "Focus on the Family," tape series (Waco, TX: Word, 1978).

12. Elisa Morgan and Carol Kuykendall, *What Every Mom Needs* (Grand Rapids, MI: Zondervan, 1995), 27.

13. Covey, *The Seven Habits of Highly Effective People,* 129.

14. H. Norman Wright, *Family Is Still a Great Idea* (Ann Arbor, MI: Servant, 1992), 268.

15. William and Nancie Carmichael, *601 Quotes About Marriage & Family* (Wheaton, IL: Tyndale House, 1998), 131.

16. Edith Schaeffer, *What Is a Family?* (Old Tappan, NJ: Revell, 1975), 210.

17. Rolfe Kerr as quoted in Covey, *The Seven Habits of Highly Effective People,* 106–7.

18. J.P. and April Kent, Wedding Letter, September 5, 1998.

19. Karen Scalf Linamen, "Family with a Purpose," *Today's Christian Woman* (July/August 1998): 56.

20. Linamen, "Family with a Purpose."

21. Edith Schaeffer as quoted in Carmichael, *601 Quotes About Marriage & Family,* 260.

22. Billy Graham as quoted in Carmichael, *601 Quotes About Marriage & Family,* 222.

23. Gloria Gaither as quoted in *Joy for the Journey,* edited by Terri Gibbs (Waco, TX: Word, 1997), 137.

24. Anonymous. Taken from a framed wall hanging.

25. Adapted from H. Norman Wright, *The Secrets of a Lasting Marriage* (Ventura, CA: Regal, 1995), 77–79. Used by permission.

26. Dolores Curran, *Traits of a Healthy Family* (Minneapolis, MN: Winston Press, 1983), Table of Contents.

27. Tim Kimmel as quoted in Wright, *Family Is Still a Great Idea*, 272.

28. Adapted from Linamen, "Family with a Purpose," 55–57.

29. Elisa Morgan, *Mom's Devotional Bible* (Grand Rapids, MI: Zondervan, 1996), 261.

30. Elisa Morgan and Carol Kuykendall, *What Every Child Needs* (Grand Rapids, MI: Zondervan, 1997), 231.

31. Cloud and Townsend, *Raising Great Kids*, 31–32.

32. Larry Burkett as quoted in Ginger Ross Biss, "'Til Debt Do Us Part," *Virtue* (March/April 1998): 31, 33.

33. Danna Gehrke White, "Plan Finances Before Weddings," *Sunday Camera* (July 5, 1998): 2B.

CHAPTER SIX

1. Billy Graham, "Let God Design Your Marriage," *Decision* (May 1998): 2.

2. Neil Clark Warren, Ph.D., *Forever My Love* (Wheaton, IL: Tyndale House, 1998). All rights reserved. International copyright secured. Used by permission.

3. David and Heather Kopp, *Love Stories God Told* (Eugene, OR: Harvest House, 1998), 15.

4 Brent Curtis and John Eldredge, *The Sacred Romance* (Nashville, TN: Nelson, 1997), 97.

5. H. Norman Wright, *The Secrets of a Lasting Marriage* (Ventura, CA: Regal, 1995), 154. Used by permission.

6. Donald R. Harvey, *The Spiritually Intimate Marriage* (Grand Rapids, MI: Revell, 1991), 24.

7. Diane Komp as quoted in Elizabeth Moll Stalcup, "Glimpses of Grace," *Virtue* (March/April 1998).

8. Les and Leslie Parrott, *Love Is . . .* (Grand Rapids, MI: Zondervan, 1999), 60. Used by permission.

9. Henri J. M. Nouwen, *Here and Now* (New York, NY: Crossroad Publishing, 1994), 45.

10. Andrew Greely as quoted in Les and Leslie Parrott, *Bring Home the Joy* (Grand Rapids, MI: Zondervan, 1998), 200, 202.

11. Les and Leslie Parrott as quoted in William and Nancie Carmichael, *601 Quotes About Marriage & Family* (Wheaton, IL: Tyndale House, 1998), 30–31.

12. Robert Levenson as quoted in Joannie M. Schrof, *U.S. News & World Report* (February 21, 1994).

13. Wright, *The Secrets of a Lasting Marriage*, 174.

14. Neil Clark Warren, Ph.D., *Learning to Live with the Love of Your Life and Loving It,* previously titled *The Triumphant Marriage* (Colorado Springs, CO: Focus on the Family, 1995), 26. All rights reserved. International copyright secured. Used by permission.

15. Wright, *The Secrets of a Lasting Marriage*, 172.

16. Phyllis Wallace, "Love Starts Here," *Phyllis & Friends* (January 1999): 1.

17. Wright, *The Secrets of a Lasting Marriage*, 175.

18. Wright, *The Secrets of a Lasting Marriage*, 175.

19. Wright, *The Secrets of a Lasting Marriage*, 179–80.

20. Warren, *Learning to Live with the Love of Your Life*, 22–23.

21. Ginger Ross Biss, "'Till Debt Do Us Part," *Virtue* (March/April 1998): 32.

22. Warren, *Learning to Live with the Love of Your Life*, 150.

23. Wright, *The Secrets of a Lasting Marriage*, 174.

24. Wright, *The Secrets of a Lasting Marriage*, 176.

25. Kenneth Chafin, *Is There a Family in the House?* (Waco, TX: Word, 1978), 64–65. Used by permission.

26. Parrott, *Love Is...,* 79–80. Used by permission.

27. Wright, *The Secrets of a Lasting Marriage*, 156–57.

28. Paul Tournier, *To Understand Each Other* (Atlanta, GA: John Knox, 1967), 59.

29. Adapted from Jo Berry, *Beloved Unbeliever* (Grand Rapids, MI: Zondervan, 1981), 134–42. Used by permission.

30. Michael Fanstone, *Unbelieving Husbands and the Wives Who Love Them* (Ann Arbor, MI: Servant, 1994), 61–76.

31. Paul Lewis, "Faith that Frees a Marriage," *Dads Only* (February 1985).

32. Source unknown.

33. Karen Scalf Linamen, *Pillow Talk: The Intimate Marriage from A to Z* (Grand Rapids, MI: Revell, a division of Baker Book House, 1996), 89.

34. Richard McBrain as quoted in Parrott, *Love Is...*, 91.

35. Wright, *The Secrets of a Lasting Marriage,* 181–82. Used by permission of the author, John C. Bonser, of Florissant, Missouri.

Resources from MOPS

Barefoot Days Daybreak®
Beyond Macaroni and Cheese
Chronicles of Childhood
A Cure for the Growly Bugs and Other Tips for Moms
Daily Prayers from a Father's Heart Daybreak®
Daily Prayers from a Mother's Heart Daybreak®
Getting Out of Your Kids' Faces and Into Their Hearts
Learning to Let Go
Mom to Mom
Mom to Mom *audio pages*
Mom's Devotional Bible
Mom's Devotional Bible Gift Boutique:
    Candle with Tin
    Daybreak
    Gift Book
    Journal
    Notecards
    Photo Album
    Gift Bag
Mommy, I Love You Just Because…
A Mother's Footprints of Faith
A Mother's Touch
Prayer Partners - Bear with Book
Prayer Partners - Lamb with Book
Raising Great Kids (Cloud and Townsend)
What Every Child Needs
What Every Child Needs *audio pages*
What Every Child Needs Daybreak®
What Every Mom Needs
What Every Mom Needs *audio pages*
When Husband and Wife Become Mom and Dad